Jailhead.

MY LIFE IN A BOX

Walt Wallace

authorHOUSE®

AuthorHouse™ UK Ltd.
500 Avebury Boulevard
Central Milton Keynes, MK9 2BE
www.authorhouse.co.uk
Phone: 08001974150

First published by AuthorHouse 9/15/2011

ISBN: 978-1-4567-7020-4 (sc)

This book is a collection of my thoughts, feelings ideas, hopes and dreams. It also includes my nightmares. I give my grateful heartfelt thanks to all of my family, Rob, Mags, and my loving partner 'Em', to whom I dedicate this work. Thanks to my older brother Iain and his wife Yolande for their help in editing this, without whom it could never have been finished. Thanks to my daughter who gave me hope.

Contents

My name is Wallace and this is my story about my life before and after a five-year prison sentence. It will describe the type of person I was before prison, the type of person I became while inside and the type of person I struggled to change from on leaving the prison system. I will not hold back on anything and will try to the best of my ability to be open and frank about my experiences. This is not another Glasgow hard man story so much in vogue these days, neither is it another attempt at a best seller by a disgraced Lord. I was just an ordinary person, in an extraordinary situation. It will document my struggle with coping with the insanity that is the British penal system and my struggle with coping with life on the outside after completing a custodial sentence in some of the UK's hardest, oldest, most brutal prisons.

On a rainy Sunday afternoon in January 2004, I handed myself into a police officer in the south of England thinking I would be taken to Scotland the next day for trial. I smile now at my naivety. The UK penal system is old, crumbling, and full to bursting with the dispossessed, the insane, the seriously criminal, and the flotsam and jetsam of an uncaring society that has no idea whether to punish or rehabilitate its offenders. I said goodbye to my girlfriend at the door of the police office in Hampshire and walked inside. That was very hard for me to do as I knew what was going to happen to me once I was inside this system, as I had been listening to others who had been inside. I was to find that my lawyer had already made a deal and this would certainly lead to a jail sentence. I chose the first firm from the phone book that answered my call. As they were based in Scotland, and I was living in the south of England, all communications were by telephone. At the beginning, when talking with him, I felt confident; however that started to diminish each time we discussed my case, and each time I came to terms with what had happened. I felt every impact of the car crash and the train wreck that was my life following the accident that was to change my life forever. I would be sentenced to five years in jail. This is my story.

Chapter 1

IN THE BIG HOUSE

It was a rare glorious sunny day in Glasgow in May. The sun was beating down, and the birds were singing. I imagined girls in denim skirts would be walking along the streets, making most girls who looked at them jealous, and most of the guys even hotter! I was inside one of Glasgow's most notorious prisons writing to my family telling them I was coping and a memory came to me, something that my grandfather had said when I was 16 years old after the police had dropped me off at my house. My grandfather, a strong stocky Scot with light reddish hair which he always had cut really short, had told me that if I continued getting into trouble or hanging around with 'reprobates' as he called them, I would end up in the 'Big Hoose'. I grinned and shook my head at the absurdity of that. Well he was right; I was inside the 'Big Hoose', but not for hanging around with the wrong type of friend. When I was younger, I did heed his advice, stopped getting into trouble and had a trouble free life until a car accident changed my life forever. I knew that, when I was around 15 or 16, if I had kept up my challenging behaviour, I might have seen the inside of a prison earlier than this. I thought about papa a lot in my first few days inside. I missed his advice. He had been in prison at one time in his life but wouldn't talk about it. I often asked my grandmother, and the answer I would get was 'if you want to know, ask him'. My grandmother was a small, heavy set brunette, who kept her hair conservatively tight in a bun. She wore heavy horn rimmed glasses, and always had a smile and a warm hug for her boys. I did ask, but he was evasive, which was uncharacteristic of him, as he usually loved to have us sit spellbound while he recounted the tales from his past. It could have been that he had had a spell in Barlinnie, or he could have been in jail while in the Army, which I believe was most likely. There was no way of finding that out now. He had died of cancer, and seeing a large fit man reduced to an eight-stone skeleton-like frail old man was very difficult to watch. I remember I kissed his cheek as he lay in the coffin that had been placed in my aunt's room, the place that had spent his last few days on Earth. I remember thinking that I could feel the coldness of his death for years afterwards. I also missed my family, which is of course the punishment of prison; I was only allowed short phone calls and had to wait weeks for letters. Being in prison, I was to find out, was like a waiting game, with a constant struggle for life between the enemy and me. Who the enemy were was not apparent to me at this time, but all would be revealed later.

Chapter 2

GIVING IN

This cell where I was being held before my journey north to Scotland was where I again relived the incident that would have me serving a five-year prison term. Up in Scotland I would be charged, and, if found guilty of death by dangerous driving, could receive the maximum term of five years. So naturally all of the stresses and strains of this life were taking their toll on me and those closest to me. That fact that I had spent months of abusing alcohol made it all the more depressing and painful, and filled me with such sadness to think that I had basically wasted my freedom when I had it. Faced with the prospect of prison I drank myself into oblivion every night. Whenever I closed my eyes I was confronted by the nightmare of the car crash and the total paranoia of feeling as if I was under a spotlight being interrogated. This was a living nightmare and I really thought I was going insane. I had started drinking very heavily in the months leading to my incarceration as I knew I was facing a custodial sentence, I knew I was going inside, I didn't know for how long, how hard it would be, and how long it would take for the system to drain every last drop of humanity from me. So as I was drunk most of the time I eventually missed a court appearance, and a warrant was issued for my arrest. I was now technically a criminal, and on the run. So eventually I would have to face the music, and go to a police station, or risk being stopped and manhandled into a police car. I choose what I thought to be the easiest option.

I handed myself to the police in Hampshire, and was taken to a police cell in Portsmouth. It was dark and miserable as it was below ground level. There was only a single 40 watt bulb overhead, which was so dirty that it barely lit up the gloom that was my temporary home. As I had handed myself into the Police, I had prepared for the first few nights of incarceration and loneliness by smuggling in some home grown cannabis

3

that someone had given me. I never ever liked this drug, but I knew it would make me sleepy so at night I would mix it with some tobacco to get some sleep. Before this time I had been snatching only small micro sleeps as I had breached bail and was considered technically on the run from the police. Being considered an outlaw by the authorities was a constant source of anxiety and stress. I remember looking round the cell and realised that it was painted a shocking shade of pink. In this temporary pink prison cell in Hampshire, I had managed to secure some books from one of the 'turnkeys', all of which had a naval theme. There were naval bases all over Hampshire and young 'matelots' were the regulars on Fridays and Saturdays. So here I was, all at sea, up shit creek without a paddle. I smiled at the absurdity of the situation, and looked around at this dank smelly, pink temporary prison.

The bed was just a flat level piece of wood, without a mattress. There was a metal door with a small peephole so the prison officers could look through it and see where you were at all times. This constant surveillance had the effect of making me think I was being watched all the time and was difficult to get used to at first. After a while you realise that there are things you can do and say to yourself to cope, to keep your mind positive; being negative, I was to learn, was hard work, and exhausting. There was a slot in the middle of the door large enough for a dinner plate to be pushed through and the peep hole above was lifted every hour, on the hour. I quickly became disorientated and had no idea of the passage of time, I knew hours were passing, but had no idea of the time. As the light stayed on all the time there was no way to tell if it was day or night. After a while I started to feel grubby and dirty and could feel that my hands were sticky. I rapped on the door and I asked if I could have a shower and was rudely told that there was not enough staff to keep an eye on me. This seemed so unreal to have my liberty stripped from me, and have such a simple request refused. I would take a long time to become used to prison guards having this total control over every aspect of my life. I reminded him that I had walked in there and had made the decision to be there. Eventually persistence paid off and I had a wash and a shave with one of those very cheap plastic disposable razors that cut your face to pieces. I walked back to my cell clean and lay on the bed and I tried to read a book I had chosen, but my mind was wandering all over the place. I couldn't concentrate on even one thought. I constantly relived the car crash, which had led to my court appearance. I felt sorry for the guy that had died in the crash and the guilt I felt about how his wife losing her husband choked me. I wished there was something I could have done for her, I just couldn't read with the tears of guilt, shame and anger stinging my eyes. Then there were the thoughts of my own family. We were a family of five. There were one older brother, one younger brother and a younger sister. My older sister had died almost ten years previously. I felt guilty for leaving them to go to England to have a new life with my girlfriend. However after the accident I had totally withdrawn from her, constantly choosing to get drunk and lose myself in a bottle rather than let her help me and confront the emotions I was feeling head on. So after months of that treatment she lost patience with me, and eventually I lost her. When I first went to live with her, my younger brother once said that it was like I had emigrated, as I had little contact with them, and so in a sense I had left all of my family behind. As I ran through my life I realised, while incarcerated alone with my thoughts in this little cell, that I also felt guilty for leaving my new girlfriend 'Em' at the police station when I handed myself in. I was the only one at that time who looked after her and I had left her alone. The need to protect her had been strong in me, and now I felt for her, and her situation. She could look after herself but I also thought that without me there she would be vulnerable, and not being able to protect her made me angry and hurt. Thoughts of my daughter flashed in my head too and I wondered if she was OK. I couldn't control my thoughts; I felt my head was going to explode. All I could feel was the blood rushing to my head. I was angry, scared, confused. I felt like pulling my hair out and screaming. In the cell at the far wall was a raised piece of stone to sit on. I walked over and I leaned on that on my knees and held my hair tight and felt the tears streaming down my face. It was at that time that I began to realise my predicament. I was lost; my life was over, everything I had once owned or possessed had gone. I was in prison and it felt like I would never get out.

I remember thinking 'even when I get out, what am I going to do to cope inside prison and outside in the real world'? I knew instinctively that I had to pull myself together; I knew that I couldn't be weak while I was in prison. I knew before I handed myself in to the Police that being on the run was not a good thing. I knew that this would have consequences, and that my actions would have a cost. What I did not really understand was how severe these would be inside prison. I knew I was being selfish, but this is what we are all like much of the time really. We all want what's easiest, and take decisions based on what's best for the moment. That is why I had missed a court appearance, and a warrant had been issued for my arrest.

I wanted to spend the New Year with my girlfriend Emma so I made the decision to hand myself in on January and not in November when I knew I should have, leading to me missing a vital appearance at court. So all of the month of December I was a wanted man, I was on the run, a criminal. I rationalised this by thinking that I was only a minor criminal, not that important, and that the State should really be pursuing criminals that really hurt people and keep them locked up for our safety. I was to realise later that the State punishes you, has a long memory, and is full of vindictive people only too willing to let you know just how much they think you need to be punished and 'taught a lesson'. During Christmas and New Year, before handing myself in to the Police, I tried to forget about my situation, but it constantly played on my mind and made some of those precious moments of freedom seem like I was already inside prison. I thought that if I could just have a good time over Christmas and New Year I would be able to go to prison with at least one memory that was good. I believed that this would help me survive the loneliness. This decision to ignore the arrest warrant would impact on me later insofar as the prison system would list me as a 'category A' prisoner, i.e. at risk of escape and this seriously hindered my progress and any privileges that come with a lower category of prisoner. Within Scottish prisons, the category system starts with high, medium, and low in terms of how risky your behaviour is considered to be for escape or violence. While you are being assessed by the prison system, everyone starts with a high category until they have been in for around 12 months. If you obey the rules and are a 'model prisoner', you are awarded a medium category and can be moved to a semi open prison. Once in a semi open prison, if you spend another few months without any incident or trouble, then you are awarded a low category and can be considered for an open prison and, if assessed as suitable, you can be put on a waiting list. This waiting game can take a while as it's a slow process. Only convicts that have at least 6 months left of their sentence are eligible. So if anytime through this process you get into trouble, your status changes and, as a punishment, you can be held back from being moved to a less severe prison. So while this is a deterrent, the sheer boredom, the constant humiliation, and the pettiness of both prisoners and prison officers create the perfect conditions for violence being used to fix arguments that on the outside would be viewed as ridiculous and not worth the bother. This brutal environment was one that I would find at first scary, then later normal, and finally I would crave it on my immediate release from prison as I had lost the skills to survive anywhere else but inside. This I believe is one major factor that must be addressed if we are ever to partly solve the issue of repeat offending. But it was all new to me, and it was certainly not normal, and I had no idea in these early days how to survive. It would take me a long time to learn to cope.

Chapter 3

THE TRANSFER – CON AIR

While in the Portsmouth cell, a plain clothes police officer picked me up from the cells. You can always spot them, short hair, crisp white shirts with a slim tightly knotted tie, well tailored suits and heavy leather shoes. He told me he was from Scotland but he had an English accent. I made the assumption he had connections or knew his way around Scotland but I didn't really ask if this was the reason he was given the task of transporting me to Scotland for sentencing. I mulled how he had come to have me as his duty, I thought that maybe he had just upset someone and this was his punishment. He was business-like and to the point, without ever being rude. He was not that chatty, and I decided that it was not really worth trying to get to know him, so I tried to lose myself in my thoughts. This was hard for me at this time as I was still having nightmares and strange dreams of the car crash, and thinking pleasant thoughts to pass the time was not an option for me. Time spent inside my head was a source of terror, and looking around also made me feel alone, and guilty, and strange as if this was all happening to someone else. I briefly thought that I was in a film, and that the director would yell 'cut' and I could go back to my trailer, and play my computer games, and wait for my leading lady to come and joining me in my Jacuzzi. I smiled at the silliness, but the brief solace of this fantasy helped me a little.

I was taken handcuffed in a bus to Heathrow airport where the cop handed me a cigarette and treated me to a burger from one of the chains that seem to be everywhere now. After this normality and brief spell of humanity, I was taken on the plane in handcuffs, and this served to remind me that I was not going on holiday, and this guy in a suit next to me was not really a friend. Being taken on a plane in handcuffs is not an experience I would recommend, well not after the film 'Con Air' which has made everyone believe that all people in handcuffs on a plane must be hardened criminals and would kill them if just given the opportunity. But this was me, in this situation, it was real life and not at all like the film. I did not consider myself either dangerous or a hardened criminal, but here I was on a plane, being transported in handcuffs and accompanied by a cop. I would have to ask permission to go to the toilet, and I could not just relax like most people around me. People were staring at me and I was aware that many were asking the flight attendants to get moved away from me. They must have thought that I was some kind of serial killer or psychopathic monster. I felt uneasy at that time; I didn't look at the other people much. I didn't make eye contact, and I didn't want to make people feel too uncomfortable or even more than they already did. Here I was trying to consider their feelings, and I was the one who was suffering the indignity of being out in public handcuffed and seated next to a copper. I tried to relax, but this only made me feel like I was under a spotlight. I wanted to crawl under a shell and disappear, but that was not an option. I could have put on an angry face and stared at everyone, willing them to see my pain, my anger, but I decided not to. I had enough on my mind at that time.

The uncertainty of the situation I had found myself in was making my head feel as if it was ready to explode. Every sound I could hear seemed to echo, which only served to increase my feeling that this must be a dream from which I could awaken at any moment. It was like an out of body experience. I imagined that all I needed to do was sleep and it would all be ok when I awoke from this nightmare; I would be back in my cramped little room in the south of England and I would put my hand down and lift my glass of vodka and I would sigh with relief, get drunk and fall asleep again. While that was not much, that was my life prior to this nightmare. Now my life would be very different. I was to learn that I needed to get what the prisoners call 'my jail head on'. This means in essence that everything that goes on outside of prison has no value inside. No one is to be trusted. It's a dog eat dog world. Terror rules, and crime and violence are everyday occurrences. Civility is mistaken for weakness, and everyone speaks to each other using swear words to make it clear how tough and manly they are. Watching your back and constantly expecting violence and intimidation is a constant source of stress. Years of this environment, all the anxiety and the constant de-skilling and deference to prison officers and being a slave to the prison system all change you and make you fit for nothing else but prison. If anyone says that prison rehabilitates, then all it really means is that they have never stepped inside one, and seen the full might of the state exercised on the citizens who have broken the rules. I don't think I ever spoke to anyone inside prison who considered prison anything other than nasty, brutish and long.

Chapter 4

HOMELAND INSECURITY

I arrived at Glasgow airport and waited for my transportation. Eventually after what seemed like ages I was picked up in a police van and taken to Kilmarnock police station as this was close to the Court where my case would be heard. It had holding cells underneath the Court. I was marched in handcuffs to the desk where I was processed and paperwork was completed for my transfer from the cop babysitting me from England to here. When I was at the desk sergeant's area he took great delight in letting me know that my temporary accommodation was 'a total pig sty'. Why was this person laughing, I wondered? Was this treatment part of my rehabilitation? Was I just here for his amusement? I quickly learned that while there are some decent people within the criminal justice system, mostly it attracts seriously disturbed individuals who, because they are powerless in their normal lives, take great delight and achieve much satisfaction in exercising this power over their powerless charges. This ritual humiliation is an injustice, but eventually I did become used to it, and later on just tried to ignore it as best as I could. After being processed and admitted, I was escorted down a ramp towards my next temporary home. This place was old and neglected and in a state of disrepair. The paint was peeling off the walls; the floor was wet and greasy, further emphasising the neglect of this place. The place smelled stale and even though the cleaners tried to mask the stench of rotting filth with cheap disinfectant, it was only too apparent every time I breathed how dirty this place really was. The chains on the prison officers' belt clicked and rattled as he walked and echoed as he led me to my new temporary home. I was like a fish out of water, and felt totally alone. I was the only person there that night. It felt very cold and really reminded me of what it felt like to be walking into a church but this church was without the redemption and acceptance one usually finds in such places. The cell door was opened and I thought 'fuck me is this a joke'; the cell was bright pink and looked like some sick perverted amateur stage play caricature of a prison cell. The turnkey[1] said it was some psychologist's idea to have it this way as they believed that the colour would calm the prisoners. He mentioned that he wasn't sure if it would work as I was to be the first one to try it out! I hear him chuckle as he banged the door shut, and I could feel the solitude build like a weight crushing me until my ears felt as if they were bleeding. The pressure of this constricted my chest and I found it hard to breathe. God, I hated the sound of the key locking in the door. I suddenly felt the urge to have a conversation with someone; even the laughing prison officer would do at this moment, I thought! They were the guardians of the system, and I was being totally controlled by them, at the mercy of their every whim. This was weird I thought. Here I was in a pink cell that had the same layout as the last cell I had been in previously and while this was bright and clean, it was not in any way calming me down. The toilet was in the same place as the other cell I had seen. The door was thicker, and the walls were painted but I could still see the names and symbols of the previous occupants carved into it. Someone had tried to obliterate them with thick paint; but I could still make out what had been there by the impression still visible under the paint. The seat under the window was made out of pre-stressed concrete and had a wooden panel on top. The bed had a thick blue plastic mattress covered by an old heavy blanket. As I touched it, memories of my childhood came flooding back. This was similar to the extra blanket I would be given if it was cold or rained when the family was on their annual holiday near Loch Lomond. As it was usually raining and occasionally cold, even in summer, this had made a strong vivid impression on me. But here it just served to remind me that I was cold, alone, and this experience was a punishment, not a comfort.

I couldn't close my eyes for any more than a few hours at a time, as I was still reliving the accident I had been involved in that had totally changed my life. I looked out of the window and imagined that I could see the moonlight outside but the window was made out of thick patterned glass so for all I knew it could have been a street light! Eventually, and like a shock, morning came, and I could hear noise and the sounds of life outside the

---

1   The officer, who is responsible for locking doors in police custody suites, is called a 'turnkey'.

cell. The heavy cell door opened and a prison officer handed me a cup of tea. I was hungry and thirsty and I'd been having early morning tea most of my life so a caffeine hit was essential for me to start the day. I stared uneasily at this sludge that a house could easily have stood on. This breakfast was like nothing I had ever seen before, not in the greasiest of greasy spoon cafes. Now most people can't really fuck up breakfast, it's straightforward really; you put everything in a pan, and cook until crisp and slide it all onto a plate. Sounds simple, does it not? Well not for the British penal system. This breakfast had been cooked in a microwave and just looked very strange indeed. The breakfast consisted of a pale grey greasy sausage, a sludge that once could have been beans, and a very hard looking micro waved egg. I knew that I would not eat this if I was on the outside, but in here I knew I needed to keep my strength up and stay healthy, if only to beat the cold. With a heavy heart I was once more reminded of just how different life was going to be inside prison. The food in prison was totally inedible, and because it was usually made by prison officers or other inmates, could be not only a source of nourishment, but a method of punishment and retribution. But more on the food later; it's a fact that when you're hungry you'll eat anything, and that morning before my trial I was hungry, and I had to eat and drink what I was given.

After breakfast I was informed that I was travelling to court. I was double handcuffed; I had a pair of handcuffs holding my hands together then another pair joining me to a 'screw', the usual term for a prison officer in Scotland. I was escorted from my cell upstairs and placed on a mini bus. Inside this bus there were eight small cells, reminding me of a dog catchers van where the dogs would be locked in cages. We were treated just like dogs and the humiliation once again made clear that we were being punished. After I was pushed into one of the eight holding pens inside the bus, the door was locked and I was aware of how cramped it was. The guys inside were scared but hid their fear by shouting at each other and making connections and trying to be friendly while at the same time appearing tough and capable of coping. I imagined them like the dogs they were, the dogs we were, and refused to bark and play. I didn't feel like talking and that made them nervous, but I was tired and at this point I didn't care what they thought. A total contrast to how I was feeling while on the flight travelling from Glasgow to London. As I had been drinking for months prior to this I was also very weak mentally and physically too, and this made it all the more difficult.

When we arrived at the Court building we disembarked the bus and we were cuffed in threes together except one remand prisoner that was separated from us. He left the bus last. He was locked in a separate cell, and I was informed by one of the yapping dogs that he had been charged with rape. I was to learn that this segregation was commonplace and more for the protection of the staff and to cut their hassle than the protection of these prisoners. It's funny but inside there is a clear pecking order. The lowest castes in this bizarre social hierarchy are the rapists, and especially the child rapists. At the top of the tree are the career criminals with 'connections' to organised crime, and all of their hangers on. This caste system goes all the way down to what's considered the lowest of the low, and someone that all of the prisoners can hate and take out their anger and frustration at. This brutal system is supported by the cruelty of the prison authorities and some of the guards. Just like the 'bushido' code in Japan made Japanese guards in prisoner of war camps brutal because they had been brutalised while training, so the pecking order of the police and prison system is replicated in prison, with everyone reminded of where they 'fit' in their crazy punishment / rehabilitation hierarchical caste system. Everyone appeared to tell everyone else that they really were innocent and had been 'fucked' by their lawyers – yes just like the film 'Shawshank Redemption'. It was bizarre.

At this initial hearing in the Sheriff Court I was told that my case had been transferred to the High Court, and my lawyer informed me that I was facing a potentially longer sentence than he had first discussed. The reality of my predicament hit me hard. This was, I admitted to myself, partly my own fault, partly because of incompetent lawyers, and partly because I was guilty of a serious crime. I was a remand prisoner, waiting to be sentenced, and the process of the legal system trundled slowly into action. There was never any sense of urgency. The time that was wasted in this crazy system must have been costing the taxpayer millions, but this was the structure of the British legal system, and I was eventually to become used to it. I had been told by my lawyer that if I made a guilty plea that this would reduce my sentence and not waste court time. He mentioned this continuously, wearing me down and telling me that if we went to trial it could drag on for months.

Before I was sentenced and during the lengthy investigations carried out by the Crown prosecution services, my lawyer made it clear to me that, due to my no-show at court, I would be punished. The trial would take place in High Court in Edinburgh, and until a new date was set for this, I would be remanded in custody. Despite being the architect of this misfortune I still blamed him, not really taking any responsibility for this. However, I did have my doubts of his ability to help me. He was young and not long out of university after qualifying to practice and he was relying heavily for guidance on his mentor who was never around in all the time during the court visits and in the contacts I had with him. I was being messed around basically because I had messed them around, but it was still extremely frustrating. His boss was never there, and I needed everything to be explained to me about what might happen. I was worried and I really wanted to talk to him directly to have a clear view of what I might be facing. He was wearing me down and constantly tried to convince me that I should take the deal and receive a sentence less that the maximum of ten years in prison. By this time I was exhausted and resigned to my fate. I wanted it over and done with so I relented and agreed to make the plea as he had advised at my next court appearance.

Chapter 5

Now I'm scared

After yet another hearing I was remanded for a further three weeks pending more evidence to determine the level of fault that I was responsible for in the accident. I was told that road safety and traffic experts were to check skid marks on the road and gather evidence from eye witnesses. As there were many witnesses, it was all pretty unclear as to who was to blame and where responsibility was to be laid. The trial was complicated and there were expert witnesses from both prosecution and from defence about engine size relative to speed, speed relative to stopping distances and the like. I knew that I had been driving too fast; I also knew that I had hit a car, causing injuries serious enough to kill a driver. Someone had to pay and I was to be made a scapegoat. I think that the car I had crashed into had broken down, had no warning triangle to indicate that it was a danger to other road users, and this had be taken into account in my defence. How wrong I was!

While waiting in the cell underneath the court in Kilmarnock, across from me was a guy who had given evidence against his co-accused, a violent guy, who was still in the same cell as the person he should have been separated from. Despite the protests of the young guy who had given evidence against his 'cell mate', the prison officers just told him to 'shut up' as they were too busy to listen. He was inevitable attacked and I learned that he had a three-inch scar on his jaw because they hadn't searched the other guy properly for a weapon. It was a crazy thing to watch because I could do nothing at all about it. On hearing his screams, and seeing the massive bloody scar on his face, I was totally shocked. This could have been avoided had someone taken just a little time to treat these prisoners as human beings. Ironically they soon found the time for him after that totally avoidable incident. This is one reason why I came to despise some of the prison guards or 'screws' as everyone calls them. This is what happens on a regular basis and is totally avoidable. However as it's only criminals committing violence against each other, who really cares? Certainly not your average Sun reader who's fed a pile of crap daily on how cushy it is inside, or how prisoners live the life of 'Riley' and have satellite TV etc.

After this hearing, I was to be taken back to Kilmarnock prison; however on arrival we were told that it was full – hurrah for New Labour who jailed more people per head of population than any other European country. So I was taken to Barlinnie prison in North East Glasgow. I was later to regret the fate that had led to me being refused entry to Kilmarnock. I was taken to the infamous 'Bar-L', the 'big hoose' Barlinnie prison, Glasgow.

Chapter 6

BARLINNIE PRISON

The famous Bar-L as it was known in Glasgow was once the home of Jimmy Boyle and other notorious hard men, who had put this place deep into the consciousness of ordinary people by writing about their brutal treatment and their eventual freedom. I knew a little about this place, about the overcrowding, that it was full mainly of prisoners on remand, awaiting sentencing. I knew that that there was constant tension and it was full of wannabe gangsters. I understood that violence was not only inevitable, but necessary to maintain the pecking order in the upside down society that is prison. Inside prison, life as you know it stops, and you then take on the persona of someone constantly under surveillance with all of the stress that accompanies this lifestyle. Imagine that you are aware of being watched, and at any time anyone could stab you, slash you or maim you. That if you upset some of the hardened career criminals or their associates you will be taken out of circulation by being murdered or maimed. That if you speak out of turn to any prison guard, you will be punished by a severe beating to keep you in line and under their control. Imagine that this is happening every single day, and that to have your cell door closed becomes the thing that you crave, to shut out, even for a few hours, the madness that this pressure cooker is. Imagine that where once you craved fresh air and freedom, once inside you long to be locked up for your own safety. Imagine that to be sincere, to be honest, and to care for someone in this environment will have you labelled as an outsider and that this is dangerous and will get you beaten for your weakness. Imagine everything that makes you a normal person on the outside makes you totally abnormal and ill equipped to deal with life on the inside. It quickly became clear to me that life on the inside was going to take some getting used to. I knew from what I'd heard and read that this infamous prison was full of hardened criminals and even harder prison officers. It really was no place for tears and self pity as that was the fastest way to the prison hospital or the morgue. How was I to survive in this upside down world? In this system where everything is controlled and your behaviour is constantly monitored, things out of the ordinary happened on a daily basis.

Thinking about it now, the most memorable thing about going inside has to be when they strip you as naked as the day you were born and search every orifice you have. After this ritual humiliation, then you get the pleasure of wearing one of their white jump suits with holes in the arse and crotch, just to add to the humiliation. I along with the other new inmates was given a cell number and a prison number.

We all had our fingerprints taken and all of the smokers among us were given a pouch of tobacco which would be deducted from your first wage. At this time the weekly cell wage was £3.50 if you didn't have a work placement. If you were lucky enough to be allocated a work placement then what you were entitled to earn depended on what kind of job you had. After being given a number and a cell also known as a 'peter', I was then taken to the duty Social Worker for an initial assessment. They wanted to know everything about me, my family, and my associates. I told them only what I had to without elaborating. I believed that was enough for them. I believed that the State had punished me enough. To have them prying into the lives of my family was just too much and I said very little and co-operated only as much as I had to. I didn't want to tell them too much about myself. I didn't want to get to know anyone. I was like this because by this time I had been warned by the other prisoners that the less they know about you the less they have to hurt you with later. So while on the outside, social services are there usually to help, in prison the information they have on file can be used to punish and control you. It's not true of all of the social workers and other support services there but there are some very sadistic prison officers who if they learned anything that could be used to control you would and do use this when it suits them. Social workers are a little better; some are good, but others just love the control element of their job a little too much for me. So I cooperated only as much as the situation demanded. We were taken from the reception wing to 'A hall', where some of the group I was in were allocated cells and we then moved on to 'E hall'. On entering I was immediately struck by how massive this place was. I looked up, it was so high. On the left side of the entrance was a small area, slightly bigger than a phone box, which the prison officers used for their office. This was called 'the reception'. In this massive hall the cells were on four levels, called 'flats'. The ground floor was used to store clothes and one empty cell was used as a holding pen to keep the prisoners together when medical or dental appointments were arranged. At the far end I was later to find out that the most hardened drug users were put there as the stairs were too dangerous to manoeuvre in their drugged drunken state. In Barlinnie another empty cell was used for distribution of the breakfast cereals in small bags in the morning. Next to that were the kitchens where the 'cooks' were placed. But no cooking took place as everything was brought from the main kitchen to be reheated there. Next to the reception was a stairway in the middle of the ground floor landing. Before I headed up the stairs I had a quick look behind me. Above the entrance door was a large window similar in shape and style to a church window but without the stained glass effect. Looking up I could see what used to be another floor. The cells were bricked over and the railings and walkways were removed. High above me, I could see the ceiling and just underneath was a walkway with an oval shaped hole where the water jet was situated. This was used in riot situations, something I was glad that never happened during my time there. I was aware that many people had been here before me. Some had survived, some had not. I was not sure of how I was feeling. I just wanted to be left alone for a little while to gather my thoughts and work out how I was going to survive in this madhouse.

Barlinnie prison started as a building to house offenders in 1880 on what was Barlinnie Farm Estate. The bell hanging in the sterile area of the Health Centre was from the original farm estate and was used to signal the start and the end of the working day. There is an original part of the farm used as the farm manager's office. It is now the prison Health Centre and is now perhaps the main focal point of the prison which essentially was built around it. 1882 was the first time prisoners stepped foot in the prison and into what has since become known as 'A hall'. By 1897 three new halls, Hall A, Hall B, and Hall C, were added. The completion of 'E Hall' meant that this new prison could hold 900 prisoners at any one time. Just outside the prison, accommodation which housed 35 staff was added. Originally what have since become known as 'The Special Unit' was for the segregation of female prisoners. This special unit is now the Phoenix and MDT unit or Mandatory Drug Test Unit. In 1967 there was more construction in the compound and to this day construction is still being carried out, so Barlinnie is always a work in progress. There was a new visiting area built fairly recently. But no matter what they do to it, it is without doubt a dreadful place and should have been demolished decades ago.

So after my initial registration, processing and being given a number, I found myself housed in E Hall, the most awful place I've ever seen. It was in ruins. I was summoned up the stairs by a guard that looked like a member of the Gestapo. The effect was made by the cap having had the peak slashed inside so that it fell forward, so we couldn't see his eyes. He growled at me and shouted 'Get up here shit head, take a box and piss pot'. I then was escorted to my cell; thank goodness, I didn't have to share at that time, I would have totally despaired. I looked in the box I had been given; there was a toilet roll, a tub of wipes and a pot to shit in. After around two hours, the cell door opened and I was handed a radio from one of the 'pass men' – a 'pass man' is really just that, he passes things to prisoners like breakfast in the morning, change of kit and the bedding which was changed weekly. Pass men also pass in dinners to the prisoners that aren't allowed out for causing trouble. Most things that the prisoners ask for within reason are passed in but the prison officers are the only ones to open and close the doors. The 'pass men' also help the prison officers to move things and people around the prison, and mostly with cleaning out all the cells that are vacant and basically carry out most of the cleaning within the prison. After I had been placed in my cell I asked for some paper and a pen to keep busy. I had already accepted the fact that no one was going to open the door and say 'Ok, sir, there's been a misunderstanding, you can go home now'. Imagine my surprise when I turned on the radio and the second song on was "things can only get better" by D-ream. I had a wee snigger and started talking to myself. Over time I did a lot of that. I had managed to convince myself that I was the only one that made sense in there.

The next day after one of the longest nights of my life, my door opened at 7.30 in the morning; I was already up and about. I didn't want to be vulnerable in this place; I still felt like a fish out of water, and just like that fish I was unable to breathe in this strange alien environment. I just watched what everyone else was doing and went with the flow. There were over 70 or 80 prisoners going to the toilet at the top of the second landing to slop out. There were four landings. That's around three hundred and fifty prisoners, most of them pissed off for one reason or another. I was a quick learner. I had been billeted in the remand wing; it only had one floor so it was not too crowded. At the entrance to the wing was an office area and it was always staffed by a screw but, as always in this kind of place, there were blind spots where crimes and rule breaking was extremely commonplace.

Sleeping in a cell in prison creates strange dreams and thoughts that just seem to randomly appear in your mind. In the isolation of your prison cell you find yourself making up scenarios that are just too stupid to repeat. I would make up fights in my head and get out of them with cunning and speed and wit but this always made me on edge and shaky and too highly strung when awake. Then in the morning all was fine after the nightmares, however the after effects stayed with me. If something like an argument broke out over something silly like accidentally bumping into someone, I would think about that all night and think that more would come out of it. On rare occasions this might happen but usually fears are nothing more than paranoia and the other person is actually sleeping like a baby. I would wish I was a screw just to have a key to let myself out and taste some freedom. I would sit in my cell, daydreaming and elaborating escapades to get out. Then I would think it would just add more time and I was having difficulties dealing with the time I had been given already. To be totally honest being inside totally messes with your head. It takes a long time to learn how to sleep while in a constantly hostile environment. They say that soldiers in constant battle conditions are under so much stress for such long periods that post traumatic stress disorder – what used to be known as 'shell shock' during the first world war - is inevitable. Some stress is healthy, even desirable to help you stay sharp and keep you keen and fit. Too much makes you paranoid, prone to violent outbursts, and constantly fatigued. But no one in prison is ever going to get such a diagnosis. If this were to happen we would need to radically re-assess our entire criminal justice system and examine whether punishment is actually a deterrent and whether it prevents re-offending. I became convinced that prison turns anyone into a monster (and that includes the prison officers) because eventually everyone is tainted by this brutal system. Who knows, I'm no expert, but I do know that what happens inside does not deter anyone from committing crime if they perceive crime to be their 'career'. For this type of person, prison is a university. For most people, however, it is a brutalising regime that puts convicts in a state of paranoia and distrust, ever ready to be violent or have violence committed on them. This is what prison does to people. Eventually people are released, highly strung, prone to rage and violent outburst, and constantly paranoid and fatigued from the constant surveillance. Even now, a couple of years after my release, I still imagine I'm there, waiting, stressed and thinking about all of the negative things that have or could happen to me at any time.

To be honest the prison guards, overall, were a cross section of humanity, but just with more defects, and that job really did seems to attract them. One was a Christian who was relatively decent, even if he did believe in talking snakes, and Adam and Eve, and the world having been created in six days. He never foisted his opinions on anyone, so he was a good man really, and different from most of the guards. There was another one who sticks in my mind, he was always trying to let everyone who was within his sphere of influence know that he was in charge, and that you were under his control. He really did seem to enjoy his power. Some officers lost vital paperwork after months of a prisoner patiently waiting on news of his application. This is another of the real punishment in prisons.

Some people have nothing on the outside and want to come back inside when they are released. In my time inside I saw over 100 prisoners released coming back inside, as if they really were caught in what's known as 'the revolving door'. One in particular - we called him the 'heed', a Scottish term for 'head' - had learning difficulties and had a large head which he tried to hit people with on occasion when no one understood what he wanted to say. His inability to articulate his needs resulted in violence and him head butting anyone who could not understand him. He had no friends on the outside, no place to live and no money to do anything about it. Inside, however, he had company and had purpose. At times, when he became agitated, he would be let out to talk to the pass men. He had come back 5 times, all for petty crimes like smashing windows, verbally abusing police officers, things like that. He was kept on the ground floor along with the drug zombies. Scotland has some of the largest groupings of non violent drug addicts in the UK, and all of them eventually find their way to the Bar-L for petty crimes, often involving possession with intent to supply or cheque or credit card fraud. They would come out in the morning banging into each other. They would be highly strung and fights broke out regularly among them. Another guy thought he had a lost dog and kept shouting and whistling on his imaginary friend. And another who was talking to his dead grandmother. It really was like the film 'One flew over the cuckoo's nest', but without the joy of Jack Nicholson to bring some semblance of sanity. I was glad to get my head down at times or just to be locked away from this madness. Had I seen this in a film I might have marvelled at the acting, but these characters were real, and they really should have been in a hospital, or in a rehabilitation centre.

Chapter 7

WATCHING THE PASS MEN

On my second day inside I wrote a letter to my family and handed it to one of the prison officers for it to be posted. He was very polite so I gave him the respect back by saying 'thank you'. It was unusual to find some humanity in them, but as he was the boss of that prison landing, I guess he had nothing to prove. I collected my breakfast which was put on the floor outside the cell door and was locked in for around two hours. I was at this time still very thin and weak. Before I had been sentenced, I had been without doubt an alcoholic. I was using it every day, and I was in a bad way. Consuming alcohol to the exclusion of everything else is nothing more than an illness that takes over and is never cured, merely arrested. Of course it's possible that you can stop but you can never call yourself anything other than an alcoholic, if you believe the dogma of the AA. Prison, if good for anything, makes you confront who you really are, without any of the external distractions that might be there on the outside. Things like watching TV are privileges that only come to you when you are broken down and know your place in that type of brutal environment. I had time to think when I was in a prison cell in Hampshire after I had initially handed myself in to the police. All alone behind the solid metal doors you have nothing else but what's in your head and this can be both good and bad. I had no idea just how bad things would become, until I was confronted by the reality that is the Bar-L. I wasn't prepared for this in mind or body. I was around eight and a half stone because of my excessive drinking and I had not really been that interested in food while I was drinking, so I had been starving myself. I had only stopped drinking a few weeks before all this and in that condition I was very nervous, feeling very vulnerable and scared of the unknown. I remember thinking of the truth of my situation, and while I couldn't really comprehend the enormity of the life changes I was going through, I knew it was dangerous for me. I thought like 'oh shit this is real, man'. I didn't like going out of my cell for anything. I wasn't scared of fighting, as to be honest I was used to that on the outside as I had for a short time worked as a doorman to supplement my wages while training to be a nurse. But inside, now feeling closed in I was scared of having my face cut and also being stabbed to death by some crazed lunatic. I didn't mind a beating as I could survive that. In this prison I was the new guy, who had no friends and no loyalties, and as I wasn't a proper criminal, in here I had no credentials, I was not a 'face', and had no 'crew' to help me. I was totally alone. I thought 'who should I talk to, who could I trust? As drugs really were the main business inside prisons, if you were involved in this you had a role, and were relatively protected from random acts of violence. Being involved in the drugs scene in prison made you part of a 'crew'; however as I did not use drugs, and was not prepared to help out dealing and distributing drugs, I quickly made enemies, real enemies, people who would do me real harm, when given the chance. In my first few days inside, the Lead prison officer came in and asked me if I wanted to help the guys on the 'passes. I jumped at the chance to get out of my cell as I didn't want another thirteen-hour lock up. The 'pass men' are trusted prisoners who have more freedom than others - well only freedom to move around their own wing which it is better than sitting in a cell for thirteen hours a day. Unless there is a fight or riot or a drugs raid which finds something, the pass men can get out in the morning before eight o'clock. One of their duties is to leave the breakfast for the other prisoners outside their cell doors. Then the pass men go round the cells accompanied by a screw and pass the breakfast in and the prisoners are locked back in for another half hour. After breakfast, they then get let out for slop out – a dirty dehumanising process that involved emptying that night's piss and shit into a toilet on the wing. However before slop out, the pass men collect all the breakfast plates and bowls and take them down to the kitchen for washing. The pass men wait at the corner near the bathrooms with trolleys, with a bucket on it and bins for the rubbish. The prisoners clear their plates then dump the plastic plates and bowls in separate buckets. In the afternoon, if the staff levels are low, the pass men get locked up for a while but at times we were out in weekdays till nine at night. At weekends however, as the prison officers get away early, apart from those on night shift, the pass men are locked back in their cells at five in the evening. They are responsible for supplying flasks and plenty of tea bags for the other prisoners. Being on the pass has advantages but on the other hand it means cleaning the toilets, emptying the bins, cleaning floors, and passing out all the breakfasts in the morning – so while you were allowed out, you had to work for it. I was only too happy to do this after such long periods being locked up. The worst job is the toilet cleaning. As the new guy, that was my job. The toilets and slop buckets were stinking all the time even after I sprayed them with air freshener; there was always shit everywhere at slop out time. The smell was like the worst sewer you had ever smelled. That disgusting activity was commonplace until they eventually had to put toilets in every cell. However, being a pass-man meant that I was out of my cell and gave me the chance to talk to people and be somewhat human again. After a short time on toilet cleaning duties, I developed a skin condition. This was caused by either the industrial cleaning products, or the poor state of the facilities in there, covered as they were with effluent due to everyone slopping out. I accepted it though as it allowed me to be out and about. It didn't bother me after a few weeks and while I always noticed the stench, it stopped making me gag. Despite the constant cleaning, the evidence of how dirty this place was could never be concealed. There were insects everywhere! Inside the Bar-L the cockroaches were massive. Until then I had never seen any insect as big as my palm in my life before. At first these mutant insects frightened me and I hated the way I could hear them scurry in the night over the floor. It was totally creepy, and really did make my skin crawl. I did accept them as part of that nightmare, but I never ever became used to them.

As a result of being on the 'pass' I was also learning the ways of the system from the guys that had been in prison many times before. I had to try to survive and the only way was to learn fast. I was always asking someone for advice and was trying to find a role for myself and how I could fit into the prison jungle. I didn't need to have my 'jail head' on with these guys as they were not a danger to me, and talking to them was not at all threatening and exhausting like it was with other convicts who might have something to prove. I did have to be constantly aware that something I did or said could be used against me at some point and was usually ultra cautious. This is called having your 'jail head'; a state of hyper vigilance which is totally exhausting. So in short, the jail head was a short-term attitude you needed to knuckle down while you tried not to think of the long term, which only depressed you and made you do stupid, unnecessary things. It was easier to concentrate only on little things like how many months until the next move from one prison to another, which would result in more freedom and less punishment. Or concentrating on what category you can gain if you behave and follow all of the rules, and don't react to someone's behaviour. But it was a tight rope between not breaking the rules, and not being taken advantage of by other prisoners, and this only increased the stress. Having your 'jail head' also meant being like what the Old Testament bible said about 'an eye for an eye', meaning that any threat or perceived threat or sleight had to be dealt with swiftly and without mercy in order to dissuade others from taking advantage of you. To not do this could get you killed if someone considered you weak or a soft touch. This was the 'jail head' and I had to learn fast, or I would become everyone's bitch, and I really could not let that happen. So I talked to everyone, and soaked up all the information I was given like a sponge. It was to save my life on a few occasions.

One day I was doing the job as a pass man in the TV room on the second floor in the 'Bar-L' when we heard a commotion up on the third floor. One of the prisoners had a lock knife and was threatening everyone in the room with it. It seems that he was pissed off after a beating he had received a week earlier by some people that he could not take on as they were hard and 'connected' to organised criminals. He had to react, and not lose face, so he took it out on everyone around him rather than get the guys who had beaten him up. A guard and two prisoners, who had nothing to do with his earlier beating, were stabbed by this crazy fool. This type of incident happened with alarming regularity. When he was finally subdued by the prison officers, he was trussed up like an oven ready turkey with his hands and ankles handcuffed behind him and being dragged down the stairs. As an additional reprimand, the troublesome prisoner is usually dragged down the stairs with his nose and head hitting the staircase on the way for a little more punishment. When that is over and the 'turkeyed' prisoner is put into the segregation room, he receives a beating from the guards for good measure. On the occasions when trouble happens, the alarm is set off and the prison officers come running and get everyone back to their cells. I found out quickly that everyone runs to their cells as you learn quickly that if you don't, you will be punished by quick physical violence carried out by one of the prison officers as a deterrent. It was hard and brutal, but this did work. Constant changes to the pecking order, and random acts of violence by both prisoners and staff became my 'normality'. This normality is something that you do get used to; it does not however prepare you for life on the outside; the prison should really take more time to allow prisoners to adjust to life on the outside, but this takes time and money, so I don't hold out much hope for changes.

Incidents that required everyone to be locked up until the prison officers could find out what was happening and restore order happened constantly. The trouble was, when an incident happened, everyone including the pass men were locked up so that the prison officers could assess the risk. This meant that we couldn't see what was going on, and that only served to frustrate everyone, and to start the rumour mill and jungle drums. Sometimes the pass-men were locked up just to remind them who were in charge and that our privilege could be taken from us at any time. As prison is all about surveillance and power, not knowing what's going on really messes with everyone's heads. When we knew little, just like on the outside, we made things up by speculating. This speculation became the 'truth' and before you knew it things were repeated as gospel truths when, in fact, they were the fevered imagination of the prisoners themselves. This passing and sharing of information was about control. Those who knew what was going on were further up the pecking order; those who knew the least were lowest in this order. Guards would pass information on to prisoners they liked or most often feared, and this was a regular occurrence. For instance the identity of the 'beasts' (child molesters or anyone convicted of a sex crime), as they were named by people in the system, would be leaked out regularly and this information used as a source of status and amusement by the prison officers. They would tell some convict about rapists, women beaters, people who robbed and hurt the elderly, or child abusers. Being told would make the 'normal' convict feel that he could gain status by looking down at someone lower than him. The prison officers would use this information to manipulate the less intelligent convicts only too willing to hurt these people. Having someone else to hate made other convicts feel less like criminals. The prison officers also created 'in groups' and 'out groups' using this information to control the population in the prison – much like the newspapers the Sun and the News of the World tend to do with their populist stance and outrage at certain things like under age sex for example, while at the same time parade pictures of scantily clad teens barely out of school to sell their papers. So while I had no time for these sex criminals, I could see how this information was used and abused within the prison regime to control the population. They were just like Wardens in a zoo, although all of us were wildlife.

Chapter 8

THE ZOO

Early in my prison sentence, I was sharing with others, and who you shared a cell with could make an hour seem like a week. Even in a controlled environment like a prison, things happen that are not supposed to. Convicts exact revenge on other convicts for the slightest affront like a snide remark or a careless laugh. This place had its own rules and I was learning by observation and the hard way by making mistake after mistake. It was totally different from life on the outside. I found myself sharing a cell with a selfish junkie who didn't care about anyone but himself. In prison everyone wears prison issue clothes; however you are sometimes allowed your own footwear. Typically of the opiate user he lost his sense of smell or lost his dignity; whatever it was, he always smelled bad. All he really wanted was a drug induced coma every day. As a recovering alcoholic, I knew that this was his way of dealing with the problems he had. He was typically thin like all heavy users of depressant drugs, and like most of them, had been raised in a tough working class estate. This prison, like all prisons I would visit, were full of drug addicts, many from areas of deprivation scattered all over Scotland. He had a rough look about him, compounded by a large Y shaped scar on the right side of his face. This indicated that he had not paid a drug debt at some point and emphasised that he was not to be trusted. He had short grey hair with dark sunken eyes that peered out from his skull-like head. His fingers were burnt black from chasing the dragon, and I was to learn that this was the most common way of getting drugs into the body in prison as the threat of HIV and Hepatitis did keep some but not all of them from sharing needles. Chasing the dragon involves burning heroin on tin foil. This is done by holding a naked flame under a piece of foil and then inhaling the vapour until nothing but black ash is left. Often I saw him raiding the bins of his cell mates to find more foil or at least a trace of oil on it for a hit. Drugs are smuggled along with other illegal commodities, and are a very big business in prison.

Typically illegal drugs were bought and sold on a daily basis. A common occurrence was for convicts on the remand wing to sell or give away their own personal stash for another commodity, either uppers or downers if they were going for sentencing that day. This was because they were thoroughly searched and drugs not immediately consumed would definitely be found by vigilant prison officers. So if the prisoner never came back after leaving their cell, fair deal, if they returned pending sentencing or prior to a move to another prison then they would try their best to get back what they had traded before they left. This caused no end of trouble and mayhem usually ensued when junkies were arguing over who owed who, and who had drugs that they believed still 'belonged' to them.

A lot of methadone is given out in prisons; they must bring it in tanker Lorries. In Barlinnie, when the convicts identified as users were queuing for their methadone fix in the morning, it would be swallowed in front of a nurse who was dispensing it to them. However the liquid was usually held in the back of the throat and spat into a cup when they returned to their cell. This 'spit methadone' was currency and would be passed on for a pill of some sort, which was considered a higher or more valuable commodity. This was very common; however the first time I witnessed this, I was near to vomiting when the junkie who was sharing my cell swallowed another guy's methadone which had come directly from the other guy's mouth! I know that this is disgusting but that's the nature of addiction. I understood that, while I considered myself different from them, I was also an addict and my drug was alcohol. But I don't think alcohol addicts would ever regurgitate alcohol for each other, at least I'd never heard of that happening. I sound uncaring at times when I mention the people I came across in prison; however I also realise that it's their thing; it's not mine and I don't like junkies being around me, and I would avoid them if I could. I knew at times I had no choice in the matter and yes I felt sorry for some of them. On a few occasions I could sit in my cell with one of them and he would just pour his heart out to me. I mean, despite being judgemental sometimes, I am on occasions a good listener and can help other people. I found myself listening to someone else' life story on many occasions. But I have to say, the first junkie I was sharing a cell with really disgusted me with his lack of cleanliness. I just could not stand it. Not only was he smelly, but he snored all night and after less than a week of this I just couldn't take this anymore and cracked. As I have just described, a great deal of the junkies' time in prison is spent making deals, securing their next fix, or passing on or holding on to drugs, so as you can imagine they were loads of other junkie scum in my cell at times of recreation and meal times. There was always some drug crazed lunatic visiting him, doing deals as they always did. However while I can tolerate many things, I just wanted them out of my way so that I could get on with my time, and gradually moved away from this type of prisoner in order to remain as sane as I could in this madness that is the prison environment. So in order to get away from these addicts, I had to be bold, and I had to use my 'jail head'. I had to act just like most of the other inmates, and act as if I had no feelings, or manners, and think as they thought, act as they acted otherwise I was not going to last in this upside down world.

Chapter 9

FLASHBACK - THE ACCIDENT

So I guess I'd better explain why I was inside, and what had happened that had led me there. On the day of the accident, I remember that it was a beautiful day in June, I packed my car early in the morning, I was happy. I felt good about myself and was looking forward to my trip. I had recently moved down to Portsmouth and was on my way back up to Scotland to retrieve some of my personal belongings that I had left in storage, or with family and friends. It was a long way to Scotland, but I had organised a detailed map which I hoped would guide me effortlessly all the way to my destination. I had prepared some food and plenty of water. The tank was full of petrol, and I had brought along some tapes and CDs that my brother had recorded for me: the 'Roadhouse blues' Album; the sound track from the film 'Reservoir dogs' and the sound track from 'Roadhouse', I had all of my Elvis collection and my personal favourite, Katrina and the Waves singing her biggest hit 'Walking on sunshine'. I slapped my hands together and thought 'here we go' as I slid in the first tape recording of my collection in the cassette player. I was taking the trip one junction at a time, my first destination was Birmingham and I was a bit worried about that one as I had been told to be careful at 'spaghetti junction'. I was told this was the first mistake I made that morning; I was to make many more mistakes later. My girlfriend's dad had told me to stay on the left when navigating junctions so I did that and ended up in Essex! I had joined the motorway heading south to London instead of north. An hour later and after what seemed like an eternity, I was on the right track and I started to see some signs I could follow north. I pulled into a service station and had a bit of rest. I was stressed for a while. I was alone and driving a long way.

The first time I made a trip like this was on my way south. I had a co-pilot then to help me. My co-pilot then was a lovely girl from the Portsmouth area called Tamara. She was a rounded bubbly dark haired girl. I had met her on the internet some eight months before I decided to re-locate to the south of England. I wanted a move at that time anyway. Maybe I jumped in too quick after my marriage had failed but it felt so right. I had a lot of troubles in my life then with my ex not leaving me alone although I had paid for everything in my house. The ex-partners always want a wee bit of a payback. They see it as their way of getting something back for putting up with you and whatever faults us men have, which is usually quite a lot. My house was broken into twice by her greedy brother when I was out with friends. I did get the things back with little more than a phone call to him. By that time, I had had enough of that life. The worst thing was that her mum lived in the same street and they could watch me go out or when my car moved. So to cheer myself up I bought a laptop computer and logged onto AOL chat rooms to get a bit of feedback from, well, anyone really. I was lonely; all I had was me and little Figaro, a cat I had named after reading about the story of Pinocchio. At that time I was studying to be a nurse as I was anxious to move away from years in the security business. As I was studying by distance learning I was working a lot on my personal computer. In-between study I would talk to everyone, just to break the monotony. I would go online for escape and just to connect really. Soon it became a habit; while I was studying to be a nurse, I was working part time as a carer for physically disabled people. During this time I remember I only had two clients, two guys that were confined to wheelchairs. I didn't think much about this at the time, however later I was to realise just how much being in prison was like being disabled. Of course it's not the same, but the parallels and similarities are striking. You can't do anything for yourself, everyone assumes you can't think for yourself, and should have or don't have an opinion, and you are that the beck and call of others.

Life before the accident was easy really, the first thing I would do on coming home would be to get my PC booted up, feed the cat, cook a quick ready meal and that would be me sorted. That's another reason I passed my exams so quickly, I never stopped working and, as I was at the PC connected to the internet, this would continue until it was time for me to sleep. I would lie down on my couch and sleep without getting to bed. As I was on my own, I always neglected to put on the heating or anything.

It was cold upstairs in my flat and the bed was too big for one so Figaro and I would snuggle up wherever I slept. I had first become interested in Tamara as we both drove Nissan cars; I had a red one, she had a blue one. I don't know how it happened but it seemed I was falling for her right away. I eventually asked her for her number and we would chat for most of the night. She would call me in the afternoon after her work and finish the call at night, get something to eat and call me again until three in the morning. Eventually our chat changed into longing and need and I booked a flight to see her and stayed for a week. We hit it off well and I decided then to go and live there, and see how this would pan out. To say I was impulsive and impetuous is putting it mildly, but hey you only live once and I was up for the challenge. It's said by some 'know it all' that life is a river and you just flow with it or drown and that's what I felt like I was doing. As far as I was concerned I was not being selfish, I was living, not dying, changing, not staying the same, and breathing, not suffocating. It's also said that you only find out who you truly are when you leave all your responsibilities and old life and start a new one, where you find out the person you really are. Tamara's parents said I could live with them for 6 months, and as far as I was concerned that was time enough for me to get established, get a place and move in with Tamara and start a new life. I found a job the first week I was there. So this determination meant that I had a job, a place to stay, a girlfriend, a new life down in Portsmouth.

On my trip down to live with my girlfriend, I had filled my car with only those belongings I could fit in the car. When the accident happened, I had been travelling back to Scotland to retrieve some of the things I had left behind and thought I needed to be more comfortable. Perhaps in hindsight this was a poor decision on my part. But that's life and sometimes shit happens.

This was my first long solo trip without a girl next to me, it was very boring and the weather was hot. I woke up after a snooze; the time was about five in the evening. I had lost myself in the music in that place halfway between being awake and asleep, I had to struggle to get myself together and was on my way again. As I was driving a few miles further northwards, the weather began to change. Suddenly the sky was dark, brooding and cloudy; there was a light shower of rain. A sign for Dumfries whished past me, and I knew then I wasn't far off the Borders. After approximately one more hour of travelling the heavens opened, and the rain turned from a light shower to the heaviest downpour I'd seen in a while. My windscreen wipers couldn't cope with the weight of the rain, it was very dark and the driving conditions were really poor. As I was driving along the motorway after leaving a service station, I became aware of a dark shadow in front on me. I couldn't make it out at first. Just as I began to make out the shape of a car, it was too late. I hit this dark coloured car at 70 miles per hour and the impact was immediate, crushing and very hard. A microsecond after the initial impact I heard my ribs crack; the car steering wheel had hit me under the chin, just missing my throat. I was aware I was moving again, and I realised that my car had started spinning. After what seemed an age, it eventually stopped. As I came to rest, my head was still spinning, and I made a point of checking myself out for physical injury. For the first time I noticed I was in great pain, it washed over me in painful waves of nausea and sickness. After this shocking realisation, I became aware that the car had come to rest between two lanes of the motorway. Looking out the passenger side I could see headlights of oncoming traffic hurtling towards me, and I froze in panic. I tried to get myself out of the car but the steering wheel was at my neck, the dashboard was on my lap and the whole left side of my car was like an open accordion. I pulled crazily at the seat belt to try to get out before the impact of the approaching car, but it was too late, the car hit me full on. I flopped to the passenger side from the impact. I started to lose consciousness. At that point another impact from the back knocked me out. I remember regaining consciousness with people asking me if I was ok. I don't know how long I was out because at that time I could hear the Fire fighters cutting gear to take my car roof off. Then they removed the roof of the car and the driver's door. When they released the pressure of the steering wheel and part of the dash board which had trapped me, I was able to breathe. I was shifted very carefully by the paramedic team onto a pat slide and a neck brace collar was placed around me. I remember being strapped very tight when I was lying down and I found it hard to breathe once more, I started to panic as it was the same feeling I had felt being trapped between the steering wheel and the car dashboard. Despite my severe discomfort and pain, I knew I was alive and was lucky to be that way.

At the hospital I was attached to heart monitors and was given a brain scan. There were no signs of organ damage and I was given heavy doses of morphine to dull the severe cutting pain I was feeling. I was slipping in and out of consciousness, and remember very little about this time in hospital. I heard people talking but couldn't open my eyes. As I lay in that hospital bed I relived the accident time after time. Replaying it in my mind only served to make me feel helpless and powerless, and I felt like a rag doll being shunted around. I kept seeing the cars coming towards me; I felt the impact repeatedly. I felt defenceless as my brain replayed these images like a broken DVD player stuck on continuous play. I was letting it happen, but I couldn't stop this. I became aware of the severity of my predicament when I was told that the person I had hit had died in hospital from their injuries. The Police came to visit me in hospital four times, and each time I explained my version of what I could remember. On being discharged from hospital, I was free to go and needed to complete my journey to my home town in the west of Scotland to see my family.

My sister's husband, picked me up from the hospital, and he agreed to ferry me to my older brother's flat. Despite my pain, and feelings of guilt and shame at what I had been through, I was glad to see everyone. I didn't think when it was all happening that I would ever see anyone again. I remember the panic and terror as I watched the car coming towards me and sat helpless trapped inside the car wreck. On reflection I do remember thinking that it was like slow motion, or was that a trick of the mind? As I watched the car speeding towards me and bracing myself for the eventual crash, I was thinking that it was just like in the movies and that my car would explode because of the petrol tank and that, like the action hero, I would get out at the last minute. As I replayed the scene of the crash, I remember I asked if everyone was ok in the other cars. The woman talking to me while I was trapped and waiting for the Police and fire service said 'they're not so good, son. You just calm down, someone is coming to help you'.

During my time in Scotland, my older brother said I could stay in his flat for a while as he was now sharing a flat with his partner. He showed me around the flat, gave me money for food and then he went. Left on my own, in pain and needing to escape the fear and the sense of dread I had weighing on me, the first place I went to when he was gone was the off-licence. I needed a drink. I don't think from that point I intended to stop drinking and just wanted oblivion. The flat was on the first floor in an old tenement building in the middle of my home town. To get to the off-licence, I had to make my way down some very worn and treacherous old style stone steps. I made my way down the stairs, every step only served to increase the pain, but I was determined I was going to sleep that night, even if it was alcohol-induced. With each step I cried in pain, screwing up my face when my foot would land on the step or on the pavement. I was feeling very strange; this feeling was different but still familiar to me. Although I did not know it at that time, I was an alcohol addict, and I used alcohol to help me through every crisis, real and imagined.

In the local off licence I found it hard to breathe so I didn't talk much. I really only wanted to be alone, but as chance would have it, I met Mohammed, a martial arts instructor I knew when I had trained in my home town. I found it hard to talk to him, and even harder to meet his gaze. I just wanted to be alone. I felt as though everyone was watching me. I was feeling self-conscious, and anxious. I headed back to the flat with my alcohol and settled down to become comfortably numb and forget my worries. It took me over an hour to work the TV surround sound and DVD system my brother had set up. Once I had worked it all out, I was exhausted! I made a call to my girlfriend to check in, but I couldn't. I had started to distance myself from her. I realised as I was speaking that I just wanted to get blind drunk. I think that the beginning of my downfall was when I started to block my emotions from the people I cared about. At the time I didn't pay much attention to everything I was doing or saying. I shut everyone out, only feeling truly comfortable when I was alone. To be honest I had drifted into bad habits and like many males of my generation found it difficult to express myself emotionally. Unable to ask for what I needed or even know what I wanted emotionally, I tended to withdraw and become distant, or aggressive when frightened. I was never too good at expressing my emotions with any significant other and it was even worse now. I would be watching a movie then out of the blue the flash backs would appear. I just couldn't concentrate on anything for any length of time. My heart would start to pound in my chest, making me feel the fear and trepidation of the crash and the aftermath again, and again. Sometimes, I would be fine, especially when an exciting scene in a film was playing, however the pain would wash over me like someone hitting me in the middle of my chest with a sledge hammer, whenever my mind was not occupied. I wanted to talk but didn't know how; I became very clever at changing the subject when people asked how I was and how I was feeling. Over the next week I became a recluse and was drinking constantly. After a week of living in my brother's flat, it was time to return south to Hampshire. My body still hurt and in spite of the way I was feeling inside my head I did still have feelings for my girlfriend and wanted to see her. My brother was giving up the flat to move in with his girlfriend (whom he later married) and I was ready to leave for Hampshire. He arranged for the trip back and drove me to the airport. I was so messed up and I drank all my money, not thinking about the consequences and how selfish I was. It was nice to see my family but the circumstances were bad. We arrived at the airport and he stayed with me until I had to enter the departure lounge. I was sad to leave him. It was only a 45 minute flight and I was getting picked up at Heathrow by Tamara's dad. When I arrived there and saw them, the atmosphere was very tense, as they could see I was a mess physically and emotionally. After a tense journey, I was dropped off at my flat. When I entered it was as cold and unwelcoming. I just continued drinking. I saw my girlfriend that weekend; we tried to talk, but it was too late. I had lost her by putting alcohol first to drown my sorrows. I should have let her support me through this difficult time, but I pushed her away, a recurring theme in my life, and something I was not aware of until I'd had years inside, and my release from prison to think about it. I was on my own for a while, drinking, and sinking deeper and deeper into a dark depression.

Six months later I met Em'. By then I had stopped drinking and was working again. But I was different. Em' was a girl I had met while working as a doorman; she worked in an old people's home. While working in a bar we had said hello and chatted on many occasions. Another few months passed after our first meeting and I met her again when I was working in another bar in her home town. She was having problems with her boyfriend; she looked sad when she told me about him. We arranged to meet, and I felt alive again. After our first date we were never apart for more than a few hours each day. Despite my new and improved love life, my drinking had started again in secret. As I sank deeper into a depression once more after the high of meeting Emma, my relationship with my landlord became strained. I was not paying him any rent, and despite much financial help from my family, I was really just drinking and not coping. Eventually after months of this I was given an eviction notice. By this time I had lost my job, was about a day away from living on the streets, and out of desperation and necessity had started to make some calls to hostels and homeless shelters. I ended up living in a night shelter with some of the most hardened drinkers I had ever met. By this time my possessions were little more than five bags, and I remember being so physically ill that carrying them from my flat to the hostel totally drained me. But I just kept on drinking, and it became my first thought in the morning and my last at night.

My drinking resulted in me taking my first alcoholic fit and I was admitted to the local hospital. I had wet myself and I was shaking, sweating, and in great pain. I was put on a detoxification programme and after being prescribed Chlordiazepoxide (Librium) and vitamin B12, I was discharged back to the care of the homeless unit. My drinking did not stop though. I was determined to continue. Em' wasn't allowed in the hostel I was living in, so we had to walk the streets to be together. Even this didn't stop me drinking. I would drink in the rain on a park bench on my own, not caring about who saw me, or what they thought. I met a lot of people in the same situation as me. After about another month I was in the company of about 10 people all drinking daily and talking nonsense. I fitted in as part of the crowd as, like them, I had become an alcoholic. Eventually I was moved from the homeless unit to supported accommodation to help me recover from the misuse of alcohol. It was a huge difference, and I had more freedom to come and go as I pleased as long as I obeyed the house rules. I could have Em' over to stay three times a week and I could stay out three days a week. It was a 'dry house', meaning that residents had to stay sober, but I still managed to get drunk in my room and I was caught a few times, but the staff were used to this, and I always assured them that I would try harder. After a few months there I received a call from my lawyer to tell me to get back to Scotland or hand myself into the nearest police station. My chaotic life meant that I missed a court appearance; this resulted in a warrant for my arrest had been issued. I knew that I should have travelled to court, and I knew that I was now officially in very hot water, but I just was totally out of control and wanted the nightmare to end. I wanted to keep tasting some freedom with Em', so I didn't stop drinking until the day I handed myself in to the Police. It had come to light that I had no insurance for the car and that my licence didn't check out with my address; there were also other complications which made it clear to my lawyer (but not to me fully, I must admit at this time) what a complicated and foolish lifestyle I had been leading. I binged a lot on and off with alcohol trying to kill the pain. I had started on lager, but more and more I was drinking spirits. While staying with my brother in Scotland after one court appearance in Hamilton, I drank all the whisky, brandy and other things that he had been keeping in his cupboard for special occasions. He was angry at first when he found out, but later, when he accepted what I'd been going through, he made peace and it was all forgotten about. I realised I had been extremely selfish in not letting anyone know what I was feeling, and later on in my journey from freedom to incarceration and back to freedom again, I would learn a little more about how to express myself.

Chapter 10

MIND CONTROL

Most prisons are operating at what is called 'over maximum efficiency' - that's politician speak for overcrowded – and this caused a great deal of tension and little things could start near riots. I was sharing a cell with someone I would walk miles to get away from on the outside. Inside here I just had to accept whoever they gave me. This guy looked like a classic stereotypical junkie. This was of course my first impression of him, and it was not going to change after spending time with him. When he first came in the cell, I took an instant dislike to him. He was really loud and totally obnoxious and it was unsettling at the time. He was always fidgeting and he really couldn't stand still for any more than a few seconds. I remember that he became very excited at the opportunity of a drink of methadone from a convict in cell number 26, an obnoxious, fidgety junkie. Could my life get any worse I thought? I watched him as he was telling me why he was inside this time; there was just something not square with what I understood about him. He said he was in prison for breaching the peace and all he'd done was just sing in the street. It soon became apparent that he'd gilded the lily somewhat and was not telling the whole truth. The next day I found out from another prisoner that he had battered his girlfriend near to death for not giving him £10 pounds for some heroin. Like most long term heroin users his arms were full of puncture marks and he confided in me that that he had Hepatitis C and had constant skin infections. He told me all of this just as I was having a shave, so it did make me think about how easily it would be to become infected by this person. My fear turned to anger and revulsion as I began to worry about being infected, to see him as contagious. I know that this was merely a risk but rational thought was the last thing on my mind. I just wanted him out. I wasn't paying attention to what he was jabbering on about as I just needed him to be away from me. As he was talking I was working on a plan to get rid of him. I just nodded and said 'yeah ok' to all he said. I was having a conversation with myself and had just 'tuned' him out, a skill that was to become very handy while inside!

So having acquired my 'jail head' I hatched a plan that I would execute during our next time we were let out of our cells for food. That evening, as I was returning to my cell with my meal, I simply locked the door rather than leave it open for him. I didn't want that junky low life in with me again and I was determined to fight for this right. As he could not get into the cell he went to get a guard. The screw opened the door to let him in, I pulled it closed again and shouted 'if that cunt steps one foot inside here, he won't be breathing in the morning'. They could see that I was dead serious. He was moved and I had the cell to myself. What a victory. It felt like heaven. When the cell door closed I lay myself down on the bunk and let out a sigh of relief. I had my own space at last; I could take out my tobacco without having it stolen. You have no idea how this simple luxury felt to me after having to have eyes in the back of my head. Everything that was not nailed or glued down was nicked and sold or swapped. Inside prison, everything has to be watched. If you are a smoker like me, your tobacco and especially your lighter disappear often. The same thing with your coffee, and your tea bags, indeed anything that made life inside tolerable was currency, so it could be and was stolen, and I had everything stolen from me on a regular basis until I became hyper vigilant like all the other prisoners. This is the nature of the place, and it was not like life on the outside! Everything and anything was stolen, and if it could not be used immediately, was bartered for something else that was useful. I tried to keep myself to myself after gaining a single cell, and tried to stay out of interacting with others as much as possible.

While in the Bar-L, I was either studying or working, so at the weekends I started to make my cell into my home to lessen the pain of being confined for up to 23 hours a day. I converted bed sheets I had taken from the laundry room to make curtains by making holes every inch along the top and braided string through them. I had taken a table and chair from an empty cell earlier that morning and I laid another sheet on the table as a table cloth. I picked the best sheets I could find for the bed and let it hang down so you couldn't see under the bed. I drew pictures for my wall and fixed them on the wall with toothpaste. These simple things made a huge difference to my mood. I was in a single cell I had given it a makeover. While the solitude would at certain times be relaxing, it was also a punishment. However certain things were always noisy – like old firm football games. When they played, the place erupted with excitement, anger, frustration, and the pecking order and group factions were prominent. When the two Glasgow 'Old Firm' football clubs Rangers and Celtic were playing, the prison would erupt. Doors banged like steel drums and no one could concentrate on anything. I'm not a big fan of football so it was mostly irritating for me.

Prison is a total bore, where you have lots of free time on your hands. Every time I walked towards my cell I was always filled with such dread. The sheer weight of the constant reminder of how many years I had left was written on the outside of the cell door, for me to see every day; bummer eh? You never forget who is in control, why you're there, and how long they intend to keep you.

Chapter 11

MEETING THE LOCALS

In Barlinnie prison I remember one of my first tastes of fear and intimidation. I wanted to have a game of pool so I went over and had a conversation with the guys there who were playing. The rules were that you had to give the pool cue to anyone who was waiting, and there were strict rules about the order of who was next, it was on a first come first served basis, and you had to remember where you were in the queue to get a game. Eventually I was next and I was handed the pool cue from the guy who had been playing and proceeded to break the balls up to start the game. Suddenly, a guy at the left hand corner of the table shouted 'hey you fucking wanker, I'm next!' 'Oh really' I replied sarcastically and with contempt, 'you didn't wait your turn like everyone else has. What makes you so fucking special? I've been here half an hour and so have some of the others. So you can wait your turn!' I shouted and turned away from him so that I could continue to play. But I sensed that he wouldn't take this without a fight, but by this time I had seen enough bullying to realise that I had to take a stand sometime, I had decided now was the time So I turned around to watch him. His face started to distort with anger, and he began looking around for things to hit me with. I noticed him looking at the pool balls, the brushes leaning on the corner that the pass men left after cleaning, the chair at my right side but he couldn't have reached it in time. I had seen this sort of behaviour before when I was working on the nightclub doors and I could read people very quickly and evaluate what my reaction to their behaviour should be. As he was coming toward me brandishing a pool cue that he was going to use as a weapon, I decided that I had to block his attack and move first towards him and take him by surprise. As he stepped forward I stunned him by doing the opposite of what he expected. As he was attacking he expected me to step back. I simply moved forward quickly and I hit him with a turning punch which I had practiced many hours during my many years as a student of Tukido, a martial art similar to Ti Kwan do. Just before making contact with his face, I dropped my thumb back to get extra power as I smacked him on his cheek. I had thought about every move I was making while he was still on the action of picking up his weapon. I hit him on the side of his face and he went straight down hard, dropping like a stone. The other guys crowded around me and carried me in a hurried and concerned way back to my cell. In my cell, one by one, they took turns to tell me 'look mate let it go, that guy is connected' and by that I knew they meant that he had gangster friends that could have asked some guy that loved the drugs to cut my face. In prison they don't try and kill, it's best to have you marked as a reminder of their power over people. Inside prison killings are rare, and what is most common is being marked for life by a visible scar, usually to the face. Victims have their face marked as a permanent reminder of their transgression. I knew that despite their concern for me, it was clear that they didn't like this person any more than I did but they were afraid of him and the people that he was connected with.

A day after this particular incident in the pool room, I was hit in the side with a sharpened tooth brush. I knew who had arranged my little encounter. I was in pain for a while, but having become just like the rest of them, I was able to cope. All this aggravation and palaver and I hadn't even started a proper sentence yet! I was still on remand. I knew then that my time inside this environment was going to get even worse before it became better. I later saw in the paper that this guy was sentenced to 19 years for smuggling drugs. He would get plenty of chances to play pool in that time.

After my encounter with the sharpened toothbrush, I was taken to the doctor and was laid up for a while in my cell while I recovered. I was given pain killers and was quizzed by the prison staff about what had happened. I told them I had an accident on the stairs. 'Ah! Right!' was the reply. They had heard it all before many times; but I knew instinctively not to inform as this would be a grave mistake. Not because I was scared, just that it was not the correct thing to do and I valued my reputation, small as it was inside. So after meeting the locals, I realised that I would be constantly in danger, and I had to keep my wits about me. I also knew that I had to stay fit and healthy so that I could protect myself from further attacks.

I was usually fit and healthy when I was not drinking and in prison I tried to get back into shape to feel better. To be honest to try to limit the total mind numbing boredom that happens inside prison, a regime of fitness is ideal. I wanted to go to the gym and asked one of the prison officers if I could start going to become fit. I was told I needed to get a full check up from the prison doctor before I was allowed to go to satisfy the prison authorities that I wasn't taking any illegal drugs. When the results came through I was allowed to go. But if you aren't quick enough when the prison officers shouted that it was gym time, then you didn't get to go. I quickly learned that you need to be prepared beforehand, have your trainers in a bag and be ready to run down the stairs at a moment's notice. Sometimes you can't hear them or you can't go if there are too many by the time they get to your part of the prison. The physical training instructors known as PTI's are prison officers like the rest but trained in physical education and they ran the classes, and led the gym party to the gymnasium, as well. So if they took a long route and left my part of the prison last, I had the disappointment of not being allowed to attend. So while it is a lottery, if prepared and ready, you could win on occasions. It's silly now on reflection, but these little victories in the battle between us prisoners and the system were really important.

After my recovery I did get to the gym. It looked a very dangerous place, full of blind spots. This constant state of anxiety and stress made me even more aware of where and when I could be maimed or killed. However while this is a great skill to have inside, on the outside however, this hyper state can get you into a great deal of trouble. I believe this practice inside causes most prisoners to become re-offenders. Not because some Tory or New labour politician says that criminals are born, not made. These people become the way they are because of the brutality, because of the environment in prison. So while having my jail head had helped me survive, it would also be a hindrance when I was released, but more on that later. In the gym there was a punch bag in one of the back rooms. I went to that and kicked the shit out of it every time I was there to relieve the pressure and the stress I was constantly under. Watching my back was a full time and very tiring job. The feeling of always being watched even when you're not was stressful. The state of constant surveillance by the prison officers only further upped my stress levels. It really sapped your strength, but it also built up resentment and anger which had to be released. So I punched and kicked this bag, twice a week while I was inside and this really did help me a great deal.

I remember the first time I had worked out the system and find myself one of the lucky ones having been chosen to have the privilege of going for some exercise. Everything inside had a system. There were rules and regulations, some of them totally barmy but you had to work out what rules were being applied, follow them, and use the warped logic of the system to work in your favour. Eventually I worked some of them out and knew how to get among the lucky ones in the party that was allowed to attend gym. However this also required one to be nice to the prison officers, and I had to play along, even though I did find some of them total scumbags, and had we met on the outside, I would never have spent any time in their company, let alone talk. On my induction day at the gym, which I had booked in advance, the instructors checked out everything and asked about medications and pored over my drug tests. Mine were all clear as I never took drugs. Anyway an added bonus of moving in a party to the gym was that we didn't get handcuffed. As we headed out to the main hall out of my section, it was very weird being able to walk around without the added drawback of handcuffs. Out of my section was a small walk way; out of the main door to my right was the education building which was only for the remand prisoners. It was an old listed building so they had kept it and reconditioned it. To the right again round the corner was the large walk way to 'A hall', which was the largest wing in the prison. It had four levels and held over thirty prisoners on each level or 'landing'. All thirty of the prisoners on each landing would head all at the same time to the far end of the hall to go to the toilets on that level. That's a lot of guys carrying uncovered pots full of piss and shit. The smell and the noise had to be experienced to understand how revolting and humiliating this entire experience is. However I thought little of that as I headed past the chapel and further up past the education building. On my way to the gym I also passed E hall, one of the worst parts of the prison. Heading left through an old archway past the induction wing of the prison was where new prisoners would be taken when they first arrived to be processed. It was a new building compared to the other ancient brick buildings and was made of breeze block and with a corrugated iron roof.

I headed left to the gym and the party waited to be split into those who wanted to play football, and those of us who wanted to run or lift weights. On the floor on the entrance was a plastic box with shorts and vests in it. You needed to be quick to choose something that fitted but in the end we all looked like a bunch of 'nuggets[2]' anyway, with our prison dress of baggy black shorts and our tight pink vests. I had a look around and like the rest of the prison; the gym was old and neglected. The weights were rusty and were being lifted by very angry looking prisoners, all of whom seemed to be trying to outdo each other by over training in a very violent manner. This didn't look like any gym I had ever seen. A few of the guys slamming their fists into the old punch bag were doing themselves some damage. They were clearly venting their anger and hitting the bag in such a way that could definitely injure them and break something, at some point I would have to try to help, but for now I just watched them punch, listening to their grunts and the dull thud of their gloves slamming into the bag. The main exercise area was large; it had everything all good gyms tended to have, exercise machines, loose weights, and punch bags. Despite the gym being full of angry men, some of them were actually calm once I got to know them. I met a very good kick boxer who trained every day. I made friends quickly with this group, as most of the prisoners who exercised were not into drugs, wanted to stay fit, and seemed in general to be among the prisoners that wanted the least trouble, the least hassle, and to me this made the most sense in this madness.

The main thing to come to terms with in prison is that everyone on the outside moves on and we stay the same. Although we are angry most of the time, our feelings towards family, friends and loved ones intensify. They are moving into new homes, getting better jobs, making more money and taking well earned holidays, and I was still not moving, not advancing, not doing anything but waiting. Eventually I was taken to the High Court in

---

2   This is prison slang for looking foolish, unfashionable, and is also used to imply being poorly educated.

Glasgow. Being inside the courtroom it was clear that my lawyer had made a deal before I even reached a court. I was sentenced to five years and, as I had been waiting on just this, it seemed like an anti climax. I was glad to be told what my fate was now, after being in limbo for so long unable to plan anything. Now I had an official release date if I kept my nose clean and out of trouble. I could potentially be released in two and a half years.

So now given my five-year sentence, I was now a 'category A' prisoner and I had to pass the time and show them I was not a 'troublesome' prisoner. According to prison rules, I was an escape risk, a result of missing a court appearance before I had voluntarily handed myself into the police. So to pass the time and try to fit in, I put my name down for an art class. Luckily I was accepted. I remember one of the first things I completed was a drawing of a horse in pencil, which was hung on the main wall in the class because it was good, even if I say so myself. After that, I was approached to draw a lot of scrolls for the girlfriends of other prisoners. All I had to do was a drawing for them and not put my name on it. It usually resulted in a pouch of tobacco when I needed it. I never needed much even in the early stages as my two brothers and my baby sister looked after me. I had regular visits from them. That's the importance of what I had. No matter what I had done and vice versa, we were a tight family. Well we were tight due to various events which shaped all of us; but despite these tragedies which shape all families and sometimes rip them apart, losing our mother when we were very young had brought us closer together. I painted a few pictures which I hoped to be able to give as presents to my family. I had to fill out a form then wait weeks for the yes or no reply then hand it into reception where officers would strip it down in case it was being used to smuggle out information about the prison. After this process my brothers and sister eventually received my pictures. The pictures were my take on the iconic images painted by the Spanish 'psychedelic' artist Salvador Dali. These pictures reminded me of just how crazy the world could look if you could only see how things really were. If I was sending a message to my family it was to let them know that I was still creative, despite being incarcerated. Looking back now I think I was also telling them that not all was as it seemed, that my impression of life was different, that it seemed strange to me, just like Dali's paintings.

In Barlinnie, there were eleven cells for the under-18s where they were temporarily accommodated prior to being shipped to a young offender's institution. Looking at these kids, you could see the fear in their wide eyes, even if they did try to put on a brave face. When they came up the stairs, we would slip them some tobacco to get them through the night then we would clean out the cells in the morning ready for the next batch that night. To be honest, it was like a conveyer belt, eleven in or twenty-two depending on whether they were doubled up or not. We stopped getting them after a while as the prisons in Scotland became so overcrowded. So much for New Labour, same old shit as the Tories; their policies of using the criminal justice system to 'fight' crime and prevent drug abuse were punishing the poor for their poverty and merely straining an already overworked justice system. At one point, Barlinnie had more than three hundred prisoners over the maximum number that it was built to accommodate. Even the single cells had more beds put in them and this caused even more tension. During the time of extreme overcrowding, on our landing there was a young quiet lad on remand sharing a cell with a regular prisoner. I saw the prison officers coming back time and time again; it seemed that this young lad had been raped by the other prisoner sharing his cell. The young lad didn't break down and explain what was going on until his cell mate had been moved to 'A Hall'. The guy had left a huge shit in the slop out tub before he moved on, and the young lad was being shouted at by the prison officers for not emptying it out. It was only then that he broke down and told the officer what had been happening to him. The pass men, of whom I was one, were then asked to clean this cell. That's how we found out; the officer immediately went to A Hall and I don't know what happened after that; I can only guess that a visit was made in the evening, as the prison officers were old school in there, meaning that they had a sense of justice that other officers did not have.

I remember there was another incident that happened in A Hall. In this wing, a smuggler from Canada, who was seriously into body building, was discovered to have been raping his young cell mate every night for three weeks. The lad must have been terrified; he never said anything until he had to go to the doctors to find out why he was bleeding from his back passage. He was referred to a psychiatrist and thereafter put in a protection wing. I'm not sure how often this happens in prison as these were the only incidents I had heard about; it's possible that there are thousands of such occurrences within the prison system. But it's so secret and shameful that no one ever talked about it. This was just how dangerous Barlinnie could be on a daily basis.

Every day you chose what you wanted from a canteen list; this would then be delivered to your cell by a pass man. Before taking the prepared food to each cell the pass men would sort the food out, and distribute the trays to all the cells on the floor or level within the block they were responsible for. One of the pass men lifted a canteen bag up from the floor and a lock knife fell from a hole in the bag to the floor with a thud. I think this discovery was a mistake, as clearly had the pass man known about it, he would have been more careful to conceal the contraband. The prison officer saw it and locked every one up until an investigation was conducted. As it turned out, it was a mistake and it wasn't a set up for the person getting the canteen bag to knife anyone; but as few things are ever fully discussed, and if they are rarely if ever unexaggerated I will never know what the real story was behind that incident.

And so the regime became known to me, and funnily made sense to me, as I could see the order in this madness. However madness it truly was. I remember one incident which became indelibly etched on my mind due to its sheer brutality, and the apparent randomness of the violence that occurred inside. Wednesday afternoons were usually shower time; I was just coming out of the shower having finished towelling myself dry when I heard someone shouting. I looked over and saw this guy standing behind another who was sitting down. He grabbed the back of his hair and slashed the side of the guy's face so deep I could see his back teeth. As the attacker finished his cutting he looked round all of the faces watching him, then chucked the razor in the slop out toilet and flushed it away, walked calmly to his cell and locked himself in. It shocked me that the guards did nothing at all about it, they knew what was going on. I returned to my cell and thought a lot about that and how easy it was to get hit at any time for nothing more than a harsh word. I tended to think a lot about other things like women, family, friends, walking on grass with your bare feet or on sand; just being free would have been enough. But I was inside, I was being punished, and I found it hard to adjust.

After supper we had 'recreation time' when we had the chance to watch films on the projector in one of the halls at the back of E Hall. It was always dark and there were two entrances into this make-shift cinema. The main door faced the screen and was a perfect place for a target to get hit or in prison terms 'nipped', like the slashing that I witnessed happening in the toilet. The usual method of being 'nipped' was for the attacker to approach their prey from behind by grabbing their hair and use their weapon to cut front to back, and after this action was complete they would simply walk to the other door and mix with other prisoners and as always, no one would see anything. The credo of prison is always to see nothing, hear nothing, and say nothing, while always looking after number one if any incident occurred.

It was extremely exhausting watching your back all the time, and when the cell door was open you couldn't settle until the guards closed it. That is when I could feel safe from the other prisoners but I was never safe from the prison officers. If you piss them off, be prepared for a visit from them. This in fact was a regular occurrence. We heard some poor guy getting a beating; we could hear the screams, and all the prisoners would kick the doors in protest. It never worked though; we were scum to them and tools to relieve their boredom, or to help them cope with being so insignificant and powerless on the outside. Sometimes other prisoners discussed what it takes to become like the guards, they would say that it's the people they recruit who are animals, others said that it's the prison itself that turns us all into animals. It was hard to be objective about these bastards when so many of them lived to hurt and humiliate us.

Some people believe that prison solves some of society's ills, by locking people up either to teach them a lesson, or to deter them from ever committing a criminal act again. To them I have to ask, what good is an environment of fear and hate? What does this actually teach people? The extreme stress of surviving inside and being in a constant state of extreme vigilance is stressful, and creates many violent incidents that I think would otherwise not occur. This process of getting acclimatised is known as having a 'jail head'. This is, I think, a bit like getting your 'sea legs' only with less vomit. Once you acclimatise and become hyper vigilant and constantly in a state of extreme readiness to protect yourself, they release you onto an unsuspecting world where having a 'jail head' will create once more situations that might not otherwise occur. I truly believe that this is one of the prime causes of recidivism, and is in part preventable. For any prisoner who is being released, being 'normal' again outside is hard because you will have a 'jail head' on for a while, and are distant with everyone, thinking that they have an ulterior motive for being nice or helping you. Inside, you find it very hard to trust prisoners, and more importantly the prison staff. It's so easy to have arguments and disagreements with people you see every day and night for months or years at a time.

Proper recreation facilities could help reduce incidences of violence in prison. Some prisons are better than others in this respect. Some do have excellent recreation facilities and create chances to learn with access to education and real meaningful work. However some prisons are businesses and many prisoners are forced to work in prison to make goods that are sold outside the prison system. In some prisons there are great facilities, and in others there are few. This inequality and lack of minimum standards means that some prisoners are being treated very differently from others. So like the NHS, the prison system is also a postcode lottery where resources are not uniformly distributed nationally.

The best thing in my opinion about the cells in Barlinnie was the writing on the walls. It is a fact that mankind has evolved the ability to think abstractly, and that artefacts can be a rich source of information about who created them; they mean that we can learn from the experiences of others. We pass down this knowledge to future generations through leaving them writings or drawings or sculptures in the form of art. Some art is of course elitist, and there are many who think that the uneducated are unable to decode the meanings in art. Others think that elites are not required to decode art for us, in the same way that priests are not required to decode god, and that everyone can with the right conditions be taught to appreciate beauty, and meaning in anything. Art can sometimes challenge dominant elitist ideology of the ruling classes and can celebrate the rich culture of the artist. These marks left by previous generations of prisoners were rich in their meaning; they were to my mind an art form. Sometimes the inscriptions made me laugh, sometimes cry, always they moved me in some way. Sometimes poetry would be written, rich with meaning, ironic, challenging, and reading it such a great way to pass the time. Sometimes the symbols really were just graffiti. But as they say one man's meat is another man's poison; one man's freedom fighter is another man's terrorist. One man's artist is another man's criminal causing damage to property.

While in Barlinnie I learned about the longer term residents, both prisoners and guards. There was a guy in a wheelchair that was described as having 'done some dodgy shit in his life'. He had been very violent and had stabbed a few prisoners while serving his sentence. It was said this is why he was in a sitting position for the rest of his life, as someone had taken retribution and put him there, with a carefully chosen stab wound to his spine. I was told he was dangerous many times and people would speak about him in hushed and reverential tones. I was told never to bend down or sit next to him. He had slashed a few prisoners who got too close to him. It was as if he was our own personal live Hannibal Lector here in our prison! Like the character in the book and films he appeared to have plenty of patience and would wait for months at a time to exact revenge. He was housed in a cell that was almost twice the normal size of the average cell as there wasn't a cell big enough to hold him because of his wheelchair. Despite people tip toeing around him I decided to try to find out if what was said about him was true. I did talk to him when the opportunity arose and he seemed ok but he had a distant cold demeanour about him that made me uneasy. I could see in his eyes that he'd committed terrible things. But I was curious and wanted to know everything about people and their habits, and this also helped curb the boredom that I constantly suffered from. As he was living in the cell that had been used to hang prisoners sentenced to death it still had the trap doors; this was very creepy and further cemented his reputation as a dangerous criminal. I did find out that ten people were hanged in this particular cell and were buried in unmarked graves within the prison walls. In December 1960, nineteen year old Anthony Miller was the last man to see the hangman's rope in Barlinnie prison after being convicted of murder. The gallows that were built were demolished shortly after the death sentence was abolished and the bodies of the executed prisoners exhumed for reburial elsewhere. So although the hanging noose was no longer used, the scent and feel of death was still in that room.

While I never ever relaxed in Barlinnie, I was getting used to the Bar-L, but it was a remand prison and it was exhausting being there. I knew that a prison full of long term prisoners would be more stable, with just a little less chance of a random act of violence being committed on me. The paperwork detailing my request to be moved to another prison was faxed to all the prisons to see what space was available. The waiting for information while at the same time knowing that a move was imminent made the time pass so slowly. Waiting is all you do in prison, but when you're waiting on something specific, and the system is not in a hurry to ever move swiftly, it just generates tension, anger and resentment. Being inside made me think of why I was there a lot, I had nothing but time. And often I thought of my childhood.

Chapter 12

THINKING BACK, LOOKING FORWARD.

We lost our mum when I was around five years old, and my baby sister was just a small baby in a cot, only a few months old. I remember the ambulance arriving to pick the youngest of us up because our dad couldn't look after our sister properly and she was taken to my grandparents' house. My mum must have had difficulties in childbirth although I'm not totally sure about that because I don't remember her coming home again. She was young and had long black hair always tied up in a ponytail. My last vision of her was when she was sitting at the fire place smiling at me. She was only twenty-six when she died. At the time, we lived in a small town just outside Glasgow, parts of which were later to become areas of real social and urban deprivation. But I don't really remember being deprived as such as everyone must have been like this in the late 1960's. Eventually all of the family were taken to live with my grandparents who raised all of us. Just before that, my older brother and I were left with our father for a while because he had assured our grandparents that he could look after us. My two sisters and my younger brother had gone to live with my grandparents, who were to eventually become our legal guardians. All I can remember is that my older brother and I were hungry all the time as our dad was an alcoholic, who never seemed to be at work and always seemed to be playing music. He was a fishmonger to trade; however he was also a talented drummer. So as he was rehearsing or partying after a gig, he always had too many people in the small living room where we lived. There was a drum kit taking up the whole back part of a room, a PA system, a few microphones and loads of guitars. When you entered the room from the hallway, it would be directly in front of you. On the left, the large bay windows seemed to release light which made the metal on the drum kit shine and glisten. The white paint on the wood surrounding these large widows had become stained and yellow, no doubt due to all the smoking that took place. I remember he always smoked roll up cigarettes, and it used to fascinate me, how tight he could make them with his long thin fingers. I do remember trying to help him make one, during one period where he must have been sober, and I just could not do it. The skill required seemed beyond me, however later I was to learn as I found I had plenty of time on my hands! In the sitting room, there were two large black leather seats, on either side of the open coal fire, which was never lit unless my older brother prepared it. My father would come in drunk and beat on us then go to the bedroom, put his money on the bedside table. He was always drinking, he never cooked for us, or if he did it, it was always too salty and we couldn't eat it. He seemed to put loads of salt in his food as he smoked and drank constantly and probably couldn't taste it. We were hungry all the time, uncared for, unwashed and at this time unloved. We seemed to be just a hassle to him, and the way he treated us was appalling now that I think about it. One day he shouted for me in the middle of the night and demanded that I stand next to the bed. I was naked and frightened, I stood there for hours cold and shivering, until my older brother came in and whispered 'come on, let's go'. I remember being frightened of disobeying our father and said to my older brother 'go away', you'll wake him up' as I pointed nervously at the sleeping drunk in bed. Eventually I moved, put on shorts, a vest and shoes that were too big for me and we headed out the window. We made our escape to our grandfather's, who was so appalled at our condition that we were taken from our father and raised by our grandparents from that day onwards. But the scars of childhood are slow to heal. Being abandoned and being physically and psychologically abused by a parent leaves many wounds. All of which are given to you as an explanation for what happened to me, but not as an excuse.

Prison stories are made up of half-truths and rumours, for example, someone could get a scrape on the arm and by the end of the week a story would circulate that he was stabbed fifteen times. Some of the stories that prisoners told each other about why they were in prison were straight out of a comic book. I will give you an example of one person's version of how he converted an initial sentence of just six months to five years in the space of a few months. It started with him fighting in the street after a particularly wild and crazy drinking spree. He was alone and took on 5 guys and beat all but one of the guys he was fighting who just happened to be a body building ex-marine. The prisoner telling me this story was barely 5 foot, with a very thin frame and he had a skull like head with sunken eyes. He sounded very weak due to his drug abuse but I listened to him anyway. There were four of us chatting with him and we all looked at each other with every lie he told. So he continues with his story, telling us about when he was arrested and was take to gets to court. Obviously he was given bail, went out that weekend and jumped on a police car and proceeded to beat up three cops. He told us of how his masterful fighting skill resulted in breaking a coppers arm, the other's jaw with one punch, and drop kicked the other one to the floor! Meanwhile having been sprayed with mace and hit with batons he still managed to break free from an arm lock while being pinned to the ground by one of the cops kneeling on his back. However despite his superior fighting skills he was eventually subdued and bundled into a police car. He stood informing us with a totally straight face that he was taken to the police station still in one piece, and when set free from his hand cuffs saw an opportunity to hit the desk sergeant with a punch and bite another officer in the arm. His prowess as he described it was extremely entertaining, but just totally cracked us up as he looked as if he could not lift anything heavier than a pencil. We did find out later as we always did as nothing is ever kept secret in prison, that he had robbed an old man at knife point for his pension to feed his drug habit. These stories were entertaining, but none of them were to be believed. My story was just so banal that often I wished I could say that I robbed a bank, but it was just not worth the bother and I usually left my story being told by others that knew me. It saved time, and meant I did not have to embellish anything. I was coming to terms with my back story; however the pain and the guilt were still with me, and continue to stay with me even now.

After a few months inside, I started to put my life into some semblance of order and sorted issues into various levels of priority. I took my brother's advice and made a series of appointments with the prison dentist to fix the teeth that had decayed due to my excessive drinking and neglect. I had some fillings completed; had a few crowns replaced and had them all polished. All this work had them looking great, and me smiling more than I had remembered in a long time. I looked in the mirror and saw the smile of a film star. Then one day I had an argument with a prisoner about nothing really, he wanted tobacco and I wouldn't give it to him. I had helped him out once before and told him then it was just that once. He head butted me in the mouth outside the pass men's TV room. I grabbed him in there and kicked the shit out of him and left him lying there. The prison officers knew because I had to go to the hospital wing as I had lost my two front teeth. I sort of lost the plot after that and didn't give a toss about anything – my 'jail head' had taken over. I wanted to move to another prison after that as Barlinnie is only a short time prison and most of the people in this remand prison were volatile, dangerous, and because they were scared, dangerous in a fight, as blind terror makes people damage others as they are so frightened. I had five years of this to look forward to and the thought depressed me. Most of the prisoners were remanded in prison for background reports prior to their trial or sentencing proper. Most of them just constantly cried about being in a few months. I had years to look forward to. I was sick of listening about their lives and helping them write letters to the girlfriends whom they had promised the world to. Often the letter was the same old thing, with the same old story. Them being sorry for doing again what they always did, like committing some sort of crime and taking or selling drugs, all of which just messed them up. I know it's an addiction but it was so annoying listening to the same old stories every day, when they were only in for a few weeks. It seemed to me that being an addict was very convenient as an excuse for how they lived their life, without having to be responsible for anything.

You can learn more in prison than you ever can on the street; you can get drugs easier in there than anywhere outside. When you are on the outside, you need to make a call then get into your car, or a taxi, or bus, to go and get your supply. In prison it's in the next cell, or the next landing, it really could not be easier. I think this is another reason that prisoners turn to drugs. It's so easy to get them. Sometimes it doesn't even take money, you can use food from your canteen as currency and order and pay for drugs in this manner, sometimes you could pay using tobacco or sweets; always the drugs would be given and paid for later. This credit system was the source of much of the random acts of violence that occurred inside too. When addicts ordered drugs that they could not pay for they were stabbed or slashed. If their creditors could not get access to the prisoners who owed them money, then a family member or associate was threatened and if they did not pay they could be attacked too. So it was hard to watch this occurring on a daily basis. But this is the currency in prison, and when there were attempts at controlling this, the atmosphere that existed without drugs made it almost impossible for the prison to run at all. So often we were aware that drugs could be stopped, but the costs were high and the guards merely turned a blind eye to it. But soon I would would be moving away from this Glasgow prison, and further up north, where the air was cleaner, but the prison just as dirty.

Chapter 13

GLENOCHIL PRISON

I knew immediately on entering its high walls that I would hate this place even more than the infamous Bar-L. I could feel the tension in the air of this place. There had been a riot before I arrived there. A full wing had been set on fire, and some people were killed; the fire service had arrived too late to save them because of the intensity of the fire and the barricades erected by the prisoners during their protest had also hindered their rescue. I had not been there long when inevitably I started to argue with the locals. Most were out to prove just how hard they were, and were bullying people and taking things from them. One of the old prisoners had tobacco taken from him, he soon had it returned to him and the prisoner who had stolen it went to the infirmary full of holes, obviously a guy not to be messed with. While I was becoming used to random acts of violence, and I was developing a jail head, I was still able to feel revulsion and fear, but always made sure that no none ever saw this emotion in me, as it would have been exploited, and I would have been at risk of being maimed just because someone thought they could as I was weak and vulnerable.

While here I was aware that many prisoners had visitors, and while my family did visit regularly, I was always hoping for a visit from my girlfriend, who was still living in Hampshire. I asked about my transfer to England and was informed that my request had not been completed properly so I had to fill in more paperwork and was told to wait another six weeks. The bureaucracy was mind numbing and reminded me of the absurdity of the aliens called the 'Zogons' in Douglas Adams book 'The Hitchhiker's Guide to the Galaxy', with their fetish for rules, regulations and paperwork. Everything was about order, correction, punishment, rules, and regulations. Someone once said that bureaucracy is the 'iron cage of rationalisation', where sticking to the rules created absurdities, a bit like the lorry driver who sticks to the directions the 'sat-nav' is giving him, only to find himself driving into a river, or down a one way street, because he is following the rules, not using his critical reasoning ability. In fact the rules and regulations created chaos sometimes, other times, if you waited long enough you eventually saw some order emerge from the chaos. Only occasionally could I see the funny absurdities in the system, mostly it did what it was supposed to do, make prisoners feel powerless.

One day during my first week in my new home, while in a work party, one of the prison guards said I had to go with him to the office. I wondered what I had done and started to imagine what punishments could be given to me for the crimes I must surely be guilty of. Prison does that to you. Even if you were innocent, you were made to feel guilty about everything. There wasn't a word uttered until the office door closed behind him; he told me to sit down, that he had some bad news for me. I don't know what I was expecting to hear, and my mind was a blank I remember. I was kind of relieved when he said in a very sad manner that my dad had passed away. I didn't know at that time how to feel really. I didn't hate him, and for years I had felt guilty at not feeling love for him; I was just left with a sense of feeling sad but mostly empty. I was told the funeral was to be held a few days later, that my brother was arranging everything and that I would be allowed to attend the funeral. To be fair the prospect of release, even for a funeral, was, as far as I was concerned, a result and a taste of freedom. I had a few days out of the usual prison regime to gather my thoughts and was left well alone. I still didn't know how I felt about it all. It was so weird; I think because I was locked up and couldn't talk to anyone about it, I had nothing to compare it with, no one to bounce my thoughts off. I certainly wouldn't show emotion in a place like this; if I had it would be used against me. Every little chink in your armour that is carefully assembled over many months and years inside is worth nothing if you let anyone see where the weakness is. So I was always careful as I had seen really tough characters crack inside because some low life had found something that could be used as a psychological weapon to wear them down. Often this was not done out of anything other than boredom and to exercise some power, because we really had none. I made use of my time by sorting out my cell, and attempting to make it more liveable and stamp my personality on it. I had hung some curtains that I had made out of a bed sheet. I laid a towel on the work surface next to my sink and put my toiletries on there to make the place feel as if it was mine. I had a TV; I intended to go to art workshops and make myself some clay ornaments for my new home. I had the bunk made every morning and set the top sheet to hang longer over one side to keep my box of papers, letters, drawings, tobacco and other personal items out of view from thieving and prying eyes. The cell layout in Glenochil prison was different from Barlinnie as it didn't have a toilet on entering. To the left was a work surface with a sink, a chair that could fit under it where the sink stopped. In front was a small window which opened a few inches to let in fresh air but not enough to allow anyone to fit through it. It had a welded plate over the outside again to deter an escape attempt. To the right was the bunk which was solidly bolted to the floor against the wall. It was small featureless and thoroughly depressing, but it was mine and I hung a few posters on the wall of Mohammed Ali and Bruce Lee. I also had completed an A3 size drawing of Henrik Larsson, a Celtic football player.

On the day of my fathers' funeral, I was escorted down to the reception and placed in a waiting suite. I know it was a funeral I was going to but I was excited at the opportunity to see my family and be free temporarily on the outside. After a long and uncomfortable journey, I arrived at the crematorium in my home town. I was accompanied by two prison officers but only one came in with me to attend the ceremony. He put on what he called a dog chain, around 4 feet of chain. It was weird enough meeting my family as a prisoner and I did not want to look even more out of place by shuffling like an inmate at Guantanamo bay. I looked like a caged animal and I could see people looking out the window of the waiting area. I was embarrassed and became upset and told them to put me in handcuffs right away. I didn't feel hard or tough or famous for having the guards around me. I wanted the ground to open up and swallow me. With the shame was an accompanying feeling of nausea borne of embarrassment. It was weird to be there like that, but thankfully the service' was short. As I looked at my family I knew I wasn't the only one who didn't know how or what to feel for this man who was our father but was nevertheless a stranger to all of us. I had a tear but it wasn't as upsetting as it would have been if we were close to our father. I was trying to act as normal as possible under the circumstances and everyone was great. It was good to see everyone again but, as I expected, my day trip was over in minutes and I was back in the van and immediately taken back north to Glenochil Prison.

The only thing I liked about Glenochil was the opportunity to access some education; I did as much as I could to stay out of the work party as there was always tension in work parties, and therefore being in with other prisoners who liked education meant there was less chance of a violent incident occurring. One time while a member of one of the work parties, I saw this guy bludgeoned with a claw hammer on the side of his skull. What a mess, there was blood everywhere. Another time I witnessed a prisoner being hit on the nose with the back end of a saw; this resulted in his nose almost being sliced off. The main factor in much of the violence that occurs in prison was the consumption of homemade alcohol, or 'hooch'. Drinking this lethal brew caused tensions and perceived slights to appear more serious and important than they might normally be, even in prison. The hooch was made every week there. It's made with pure orange juice, grapefruit juice, apple juice, some sugar and yeast that you could be purchased from prisoners in the cooking party. Alternatively, a loaf of bread was also used in emergencies when fruit juice was not available. Mixing this mess together and keeping it in a tub for nine days caused the yeast and sugar to convert to alcohol, the chemical processes resulted in some very unpleasant gasses being released which were a source both of much amusement because everyone could smell it, even the guards, and much tension because if it was identified that it was in a particular cell, it could be stolen. This homemade brew could be made and stored in leftover protein tubs used by the body builders, or anything that had a lid really. The hooch was extremely fragrant and its unmistakable odour of ethyl alcohol could be overpowering; so most of the time air fresheners were used to mask the strong odour. These tubs of homemade alcohol were usually hidden under the bed or behind the sink panels in a cell. This was an ideal hiding place as only two prison officers were searching all of the cells. The sink panel could be opened and closed by a blunt butter knife, a tool that most prisoners had access to, and which prison officers did not carry around with them.

I remember one incident that marred my time in Glenochil. One Sunday just before lock up, I had a visit from three guys that I thought I was friendly with, and had never really had any trouble from. They just came into my cell without knocking, a simple courtesy that happened in the brutal regime of this prison. I remember looking at all of them and, looking in their eyes, and I could see that something was going on. I had seen them in the afternoon at the top of the wing talking and looking at me when I was walking towards them. Now these three had never come to me before all together, so this unusual event meant that I had be on full alert – my jail head kicked in. I had a gut feeling that something was just not right. I had upset a few people in my short time there in prison and I had discovered that bad news travels fast and some of the people I had the scrapes with had friends. I had an attitude by then that this sort of environment had given me. My jail had had ensured that I had learned never to look or walk away from anything as doing this could result in humiliation, torture, or even death. In my short time inside prison I had a few arguments and fights. So in this situation where my cell was filled with three uninvited guests I had to act in a manner implying I was not intimidated. I replied aggressively to one of their sarcastic remarks and one of them pushed his face to my face, I knew what was happening and looked into his eyes calmly. I never looked away until he did. He lost face, and as I had remained angry and defiant I had in effect won this confrontation. That's all it takes in prison to make an enemy. I had just made three, good going for a Sunday, and a traditional day of rest for everyone else.

After they left my cell, I was trying to figure out how I had upset them to cause them to visit me in this makeshift gang. My mind flashed back to one occasion in particular. I remember I was coming up from the dining room at the bottom of the stairs and one of them bumped my shoulder causing me to drop my plate of food to the ground. As I instinctively knew this was not an accident I attacked him immediately. When we were eventually separated, and later when we had a chance to talk, we put it down to a misunderstanding, and agreed that we would not be enemies. I then remembered another incident that had happened with one of them in the gym. I had been using the weights and a guy came up to me and asked when I would be finished. I said 'two sets and I will give you a shout'. He came back when I put them down after the first set and took them away. He had either clearly misunderstood me, or was just being impatient, and considered himself hard enough to get away with this. I walked over to where he was sitting on a work bench and said 'do you mind?' and lifted them from where he placed them in front of him. He stood up and walked towards me and, using his head as a battering ram, he forcefully pushed my head back with his. I dropped the weights and asked to see him later. While nothing came of that incident, the build up of tension had not been released. Someone must have seen or heard this and told the prison officers as that evening two prison officers searched my cell for weapons; I never needed weapons and used my fists and feet to defend myself. I had no reputation, I was not a hard man whatever that is, but I knew how to defend myself, and I was never ever going to be bullied any more than I needed to be while in prison. At about nine o'clock that Sunday evening we had been told to return to our respective cells. I didn't sleep much that night thinking what might occur on the Monday morning and wondered when something might start, so I had decided to take care of it as soon as the cell doors opened. I sat there waiting for the prison officer to get to my cell. As soon as the door opened, I bolted out and went into the cell of one of my tormentors. He was of medium build, blond hair, strong and liked to talk all the time. But he wasn't a leader; he was a follower. I entered his cell and wasted no time in sorting him out, however while it had only taken a few hits to have him in a foetal position, his screams alerted everyone what was happening. I needed to act fast before the prison officers stopped me. I went to the next cell but the guy had shut the cell door as soon as he heard the screams of his mate. I banged on his cell door and told him he was next. I could not get in so I kicked the door in frustration and I clearly heard my toe break after connecting with the steel door. I dropped down in pain and was manhandled by the prison officers to the segregation unit, and after this incident I expected a kicking from the prison officers. When I was pushed into the cell used for solitary confinement, I was stripped naked and told to squat down. In this position I felt humiliated, crouched there with two prison officers looking at me. The door closed when I was still facing the wall. I had a thought that they would be back. I waited for a beating or retaliation, but it never came. Maybe they forgot. I'll never know now.

Chapter 14

ISOLATED AND SEGREGATED

I asked to see a doctor because the toe I had broken was causing me a great deal of pain. I was prescribed paracetamol for the pain and nothing else; over time my toe fused straight and I would never be able to bend it ever again. My fault, I know, but I still blamed the prison system for my fused toe because if I had been free, I would have had an x-ray, and it would have been plastered and reset, I'd have been given pain killers and a follow up appointment with a specialist, and if I required it, a physiotherapist to regain mobility. Our country maybe going to hell in a hand basket, but the principles of free health care at the point of delivery are the envy of the modern world, and this nonsense about privatising health care, and making profit from misery is for me more immoral than bank robbery. So I had a long time to think about these and other injustices while in solitary confinement. I started reading a lot while there and the letters I wrote were mostly about how angry I was and how this place was changing me into someone or something I didn't like.

While in solitary confinement, I was told I had a visit from the mental health team and on hearing this I informed the prison officers I didn't want to see them. I was told later that day that I had to see the governor to be given punishment for my act of defiance. I was given nine days in segregation and told if it happened again that I would be down there permanently until I showed that I could behave myself. The governor told me that one of my conditions was to see the mental health team for evaluation. I asked him in all seriousness 'what was being evaluated'? I was angry and frustrated, that I who had once been a normal law abiding citizen was now being told that I was mentally ill. I was so angry that regrettably, and stupidly, I told him to piss off and was given another three days. He asked me once more to consent to a visit from the mental health team, and once again I refused.

He was now angry and gave me another six days. This reminded me of the scene in 'Breakfast Club' where Judd Nelson's character is being told he has detention and keeps answering back, which results in the teacher adding more days to his detention, until eventually he has to shut up or he'll be in for the rest of his life. This is just how I felt. While it was absurd, the reality was that by taking a stand against the governor, I was being stupid, and was only hurting myself really. But I did not understand this at the time. I thought I had better just go with it. I eventually realised that I could not win, and stopped talking, and consented to the evaluation by the mental health nurses. A day passed and I was escorted by three prison officers to the medical centre. I had written to my brother telling him that I would not be giving those bastards wet dreams about what demons or thoughts I had in my head, and he agreed that this would be the best course of action. I had heard that they put everything in your file and this information was used to hold people back from parole, or moving to other less punishing prisons. I sat there and only gave yes or no answers and nothing more. I refused medication and refused a student to be present during my so called evaluation. I was respectful but my attitude to the treatment I had received resulted in me being assessed by psychiatric services. I was calm, but did let them see that prison had triggered my behaviour, not my sudden mental ill health. I finally told them that that I just wanted peace, and to be able to return to my cell to complete my sentence with the minimum of hassle.

Prison life had few luxuries, and if you had any they were bought and paid for, or hard earned. All there was in any basic cell was a mattress, a bucket and a pot to piss in. Later I was given a radio and a book to read, that's when I started to read books by the crate load. I just loved learning. I would read late at night just with the light of the spot lights outside. I was only let out of the cell three times a day for a very short time. The windows in the cell were sealed so it was very claustrophobic. The lights were controlled by the prison officers on the outside. One guy down in the segregation unit was a lifer and had been down there for years; he had never been out of prison for more than six months at a time since he was sixteen years old, mostly for knife offences. While he was serving an eight-year sentence, he stabbed two prison officers and now he would never be released. I think hearing this changed my attitude.

When I was alone in this segregation cell, I found it hard to breathe as I was in another strange situation. I couldn't settle. Every time I heard keys, I waited for a beating. I was tired and scared as I was still naked. It's strange; I can take a beating with my clothes on but was scared at the thought of getting the same without any clothes on. I think it's because I thought the clothes would give me some cushioning from the blows. The door opened later and a pair of jeans and a sweat shirt was thrown in and I was asked if I wanted to go down to the stores to get some 'kit', ,Meaning did I want to buy toothpaste, a razor etc.. I was amazed and startled by the humanity and normality of this simple statement. It was just not what I was expecting, and I looked at the officer as if he were a normal human being. I can't tell you how strange that was. It was a revelation after my treatment from his thuggish colleagues. I asked where my trainers were and I was pointed to different pairs of very large old training shoes which were clearly not mine, so in just a few moments I had let my guard down, let some humanity into my heart, and was quickly reminded of the war that raged between prisoners and the prison officers. They had a snigger at how ridiculous I looked when I put the massive training shoes on, small minds eh?

I had a doctor's appointment a few days later. While walking up the corridor, the gym door opened. A group of prisoners came out with a prison officer and the guy whom I had attacked before was taunting me, calling me 'a pussy' and saying that I'd hit like a girl. In actual fact, he was crying like a girl when I was in his cell with him alone. So I went for him again and ended up once more in the segregation for another few months until a transfer was arranged. I hated it down in the segregation unit. The cell was very small and conditions were cramped. When entering to the left, against the wall was the bed. In front to my right was a sealed window with two long metal panels that had long sections cut from them that let in a small amount of air. In the corner was a cardboard chair and table; there was no toilet or sink, so once more I had the humiliation of a slop out. When it was time for a shower and shave, there were always two prison officers around on these occasions. I remember walking passed them with my slop out bucket and piss pot embarrassed and humiliated by their staring eyes. As this was segregation and I had committed an act of violence there were always more than two prison officers in a line when I was let out of the small cell. The exercise area was small too. The walls were about fifteen feet high, making it impossible to climb out. There was a corrugated metal roof on the buildings. In the small exercise yard I could see the sky but the feeling was still claustrophobic and other prisoners were very noisy. I wanted to keep myself to myself and was sick of getting questioned … 'who are you', 'what did you do', 'where have you been', 'and what are you doing down here'; what they really wanted to know was where I fitted in the warped social hierarchy inside prison. They did this by asking who you knew, who you were connected with or working for. It was the same for everyone so I stopped interacting with other prisoners for a while to give myself a break and funnily enough became even more depressed than I'd been before! Just like when I'd been drinking, I started to get paranoid wondering why they were asking so many questions. Were they friends of the guy I had hit? Were they agreeing with what I had done or were they setting me up for a punishing for hitting their mate? All of this was stupid, and normally I would deal with this, but, inside, this style of thinking is common place and exhausting. The prison officers also spoke using coded speech which we called 'jail talk'; of course we always knew what they were saying. At night they would talk to each other trying to use abstract coded language terms to talk about prisoners. As it was coded it had an element of deniability should anyone complain. As I didn't talk to them they would say things like 'do you remember that book I talked about earlier called Judas'? Well look out for it and pay attention to what you read in it, watch the signs and find out what you can and let me know tomorrow, alright? After a while it doesn't take a genius to figure out, not what they are saying, but the mind games they were trying to play. Sometimes I just laughed at their stupidity, but to be honest sometimes it did exactly what was intended, it isolated, alienated, and intimidated me, and I hated these bastards.

Whenever I was let out of the cell in the segregation unit, I was usually escorted by two or three prison officers. My actions were using up prison manpower and was very wasteful and pointless. You need to be let out to fill your flask with hot water, and as this is a potentially high risk situation, there were sometimes five or six prison officers all in a line watching me. I felt embarrassed and paranoid at the same time; you can have this feeling that they want you to hurry up, that they have no time for you. So this puts pressure on you to hurry up, and so you rush to get everything completed quickly and always forget something. This situation was horrible but it was necessary to leave the cell. In your cell all you have is time and you waited for that time to come wanting it, but dreading it too. The guards were bored, and they were often sarcastic and on many occasions I had to bite my tongue because a slap always happened if you retaliated. I think it could be like this for celebrities, no don't laugh and let me explain. The way I saw it, paparazzi are there all staring at them constantly, and saying things hoping their prey will be provoked and this will result in the reward of a good picture – which is why so many celebrities are snapped trying to punch these bastards. It's about power, and while I did not feel like a celebrity being stalked by the paparazzi, I do now have a certain respect for some of them that don't court it all the time and occasionally want some semblance of normality and privacy. So my treatment by the prison guards gave me some idea of how it must be for them. Well maybe celebrities don't have to carry their piss and shit in a bucket, they just talk shit for a living.

The toilets in every prison I was in smelled really awful, like the worst sewer you had ever smelled, and it always made me retch. The prisons were truly filthy and I was at constant risk of athlete's foot from other prisoners and other bacterial and viral infections from the showers and from the gyms. When I was inside Scotland's jails, prisoners had to slop out by emptying their piss pot and the plastic bowl full of shit into a sink used for this purpose. It's true you could wash your hands after this procedure, but you still need to pick up and carry the pots afterwards so I always felt dirty. I felt like this every day I had to 'slop out'.

I was let out for the toilet on one occasion and the prison survey team were in. One of them said that she wanted to speak to me; well this was an opportunity to air my views on Glenochil before I left. As she approached me, I said 'These fuckers are breaching my human rights by getting me to shit and piss in these things, and having to go and empty it down the toilet is another way of degrading us into submission' I said these things to her with as much sincerity as I could. When I had finished and she started taking notes of what I had said to her, the prison officers' faces were a picture. It felt good to buck the system that was oppressing me, just for one solitary moment. At that very moment I didn't give a toss what happened to me as I felt that I'd struck a victory for common sense and decency. I didn't really feel scared as I believed that I had put up with all the humiliation, taken such punishment, and had absorbed everything they could throw at me. But for this victory I was awarded a slapping from a few of the prison officers. Bastards!

One day when I was let out for a shower, three of the prison officers were teasing and shouting at a young lad for stinking out the toilet. I said 'I suppose your shit smells of rose petals, you cunt? The guy gets let out twice a day and is told to hurry, what you expect to happen you halfwit?' For that little victory of free speech against my oppressors, I had a truncheon stuck in my face and was told to 'shut the fuck up'. But my victory over these tin pot dictators was complete. On these simple occasions when I rose above the pettiness and ritual humiliation I felt great, but more often than not, like other prisoners I was always being punished and humiliated every time we moved, spoke, asked for anything or interacted with the prison officers. They always won in the end. That's the real punishment.

After my longest period in the segregation unit in Glenochil prison, it was time for the system to move me on. That's all that happened in the system. People were constantly moved from one place to another. The next place I visited on my world tour of Scottish prisons was Shotts Prison in Central Scotland.

Chapter 15

SHOTTS PRISON

When I arrived and had a look at the building, I had the sense that it was a cold imposing miserable place. The prison was built specifically to keep prisoners in line. I was put on the ground floor full of weird prisoners, the strangest I had ever come across. One particular prisoner said 'I think I can take you'. I said 'take me where? Piss off!' Now that I had my jail head on and was wise to the system and the brutality, this little exchange made me laugh; the threat of violence was constant. Sometimes the only way for prisoners to have some status was to beat someone up, and this then gave them a place in the social hierarchy inside. I never ever wanted to be part of that, but at the same time I never ever wanted to be someone that was used and abused at the whim of some psychopath either. So it was a no win situation. Don't fight, end up someone's bitch; fight and end up punished in segregation; so whatever happened, the system always ended up shaping who you would become inside.

I settled in quickly to this strange warped social setting, and kept my head down, but reacted at the first sign of being challenged or threatened, as this was the only way to protect myself from the threat of further brutality. I was not a hard man as such, but I had proved that I would react if provoked, so in general my reputation was one of leave well alone, as I would react. I eventually realised after my time in Shotts, that one prison is the same as any other. In the meantime, I had placed a transfer request to visit my girlfriend Em' down south in Portsmouth, and the thought of this kept me going. I once more requested to be involved in education and started to take my painting very seriously. I wanted to just settle down now and get on with my sentence and get a medium threat / risk category, and be moved to a semi open prison. Shotts prison is very much a working prison, so exercise and education were not seen as priorities. Work parties marched around the prison constantly moving from one place to another, creating tension, by imposing a strict ultra military regime As work was the main focus of this prison, I was allowed to attend my Art classes only one day per week. The prison itself was by its very nature a potential time bomb always waiting to go off.

The regime in Shotts was based on the principle of completely disempowering prisoners and denying them any opportunity or right to resolve differences. The halls are divided into six sections; each section has twenty prisoners who are caged into tiny self-contained areas that are sealed by a grilled gate. The prison officers are in an office behind this grille and only enter to lock up or let prisoners attend the work parties. There is an intimidating atmosphere all the time and the tension between each of the sections could be felt. There was absolutely no attempt in this prison to have any meaningful communication between prisoners and prison guards. It could only be because this is what they were used to. The system had everyone scared, and the threat of constant riots made reconciliation and change impossible. It occurred to me that change in Shotts could only occur if more money was spent on education, on more training for the prison officers, and more money for the recreation of the prisoners. But this would not happen while I was there. People in the prison system are being seriously damaged mentally and physically. The prisoners struggle on and the guards don't know who is taking the piss, and who is serious, so everyone is treated with disrespect, and violence and threats are used, when care and compassion could have had far better results. The food in Shotts was the worst of any of the prisons I had been in. A typical meal would be served on a paper plate, which immediately would make you think that they did not care about how it was made or how it looked. Curries in Shotts never tasted like anything I had ever experienced before; mince and potatoes and pie and mash, or pie and beans were all inedible. It was possible to order a choice of fruit or pudding like cake with custard, but usually this was suspect too. When the food arrived it never looked like I imagined it to be. Most of the time, I would put it immediately in the bin. The meat was always fatty and was more often than not just gristle, the gravy was lumpy and it was just too revolting to eat; smelling it was enough to take away any hunger I had. The only things I ate were the sweet desserts and fish and chips. The rest of the time I had tuna and other tinned or packed foods I had personally purchased from the canteen. To be fair the prison had little money to spend per head on food, however the fact that the prisoners cooked the food, and that there were many opportunities for guards or prisoners to interfere with your food before it made it to your table, meant that I could not risk eating it, so I tried whenever possible to eat only food that I prepared personally. Even now, when I think about prison food, it makes me feel physically ill. Any money I had was spent on food.

Prisons are partly run not by the authorities or even by the governor, but are controlled in many ways by drug barons. As I never used drugs, I was quickly moved upstairs to the drug-free wing. I soon learned that drug free wings are never ever drug free. Most users and dealers do everything they can to get there because this is the very place because of the relaxed regime where most drugs can be bought sold and used. You would expect that drug free wings would be drug free; they're not, just like Public Schools are not public but private. Also as the rules are a little more relaxed, this was where many things happened that were against regulations. I learned quickly up in the drug free wing just how crazy things were. The secret weapon that helped prisoners get drugs into prison was toilet paper; this was how drugs were passed from cell to cell. The paper has a piece of string tied to it and the paper is carried by the wind to the next cell; the paper can be pulled in from the window and the drugs are attached to the string and other contraband or money can pulled back from where it was sent out. As the prisoners are allowed pool cues, they can use these to pass drugs and other contraband from one cell to the other. Most of the time it is done with string with either a sock with a weight inside it and swung to the next, then to the next; this is the most effective and efficient way of passing the drugs from buyer to seller, and everyone, even non drug users like myself, had to take part sometimes. Running a drugs business in prison, buying and selling of drugs takes a lot of organising, planning and cooperation. This illegal activity was marvellous to behold, even if the effects of the drugs on others sickened me. The sheer size and scale of the operation had they all been on the outside could have been used to run very successful companies legitimately. What a waste. But at least they did provide a service, which for many was seen as essential.

Another route inside prisons for drugs is through workers in the garden parties, or the guys that pick up the rubbish strewn around the prison. Drugs can be packed into a plastic coated paper fruit juice carton. This can be picked up by a prisoner as part of the cleaning, or gardening work party. Indeed anything that looks like normal rubbish if lying on the ground or that can be effectively sealed is used. It was rumoured that Clark Gable, apparently a renowned dependent drinker, was required to stay sober while on set working. So to get access to alcohol he injected oranges with vodka and took them to work. The same thing happens in prison, oranges are packed full of drugs and thrown over the wall or over the fence, to be collected by someone who will then pass them on through the supply chain until it reaches its final destination. Although extremely risky, drugs are also passed in the visit rooms very easily mouth to mouth; the usual way is with a Mars bar: the visitor takes a bite, passes it, and then the drug is stuck on with the tongue and passed back. Cans of juice are also used. I have seen many a wrestling match between prisoners and prison officers during visiting times because someone was spotted receiving drugs. I saw drugs dropped on the floor and getting ignored because it was too risky to pick up. If someone did get caught, they would be put in a see-through Plexiglas cell or a cell with a camera constantly set on them until nature took its course and the drugs were recovered. So other methods were perfected. Of course because the workers are so poorly paid they can be persuaded or threatened to bring drugs into prison, other support staff can also bring them in. As Shotts is a working prison, many people can act as drugs couriers.

I wasn't there long before I had a fight with a local. It was so stupid that it was over a sandwich toaster; again my sense of fairness was put out. I had waited for my turn patiently and was seriously annoyed about this other prisoner jumping the queue. I was aggrieved as it was my turn to use it next, I had gone over to the kettle to fix myself a cup of tea, and this little prisoner who considered himself a hard man put his bread in the toaster ahead of me. I wouldn't have bothered but he sniggered with two of his mates at his boldness. I didn't say anything; I just put two punches in his jaw and walked away. He must have informed the prison officers as I was moved to another section out of his way that evening. One of the very few good things about Shotts is the times when we were allowed out into the playing fields to play either football or have a bathe in the sun. However this freedom had a downside too. Prison sport isn't like on the outside. It was possible for someone to get seriously hurt. One day for fun I played a game of five a side football. When the ball was passed to me I quickly headed for the goal. I was violently slammed into the side panel by another player who as I hit the ground stamped his foot directly onto my hand when I hit the ground. To this day I have sand grains embedded in the palms of my hand; it's said it's only a game, but it was not how I expected it to be.

Time continued to pass, and one day I was informed that the prison bureaucracy had processed my application for travelling south. I was told that my transfer to an English prison for visits had been arranged for the following Tuesday. I thought it would have been by plane, I was so wrong! It would take me a week of travelling on a prison bus with five overnight stays in other prisons on route to travel from central Scotland to southern England.

Chapter 16

MY LIFE IN A VAN.

The date I was due to travel south approached very slowly. When it finally did, I was first taken in a prison van from Shotts to Edinburgh, and when I arrived there, I was stuck in one of the old wings of the prison, where the prisoners that have been punished are housed. Edinburgh or Saughton prison was clearly like all other prisons and in a state of disrepair. It was falling apart. I was on the first floor. On entering the 'peter' or cell, I noticed how damp and cold it was. The windows in my cell were smashed; the wardrobe had no doors, and the mattress on the bed was full of stained marks; there was no pillow, and to top it all, there was a table with only three legs. I should have despaired but I was happy to be moving and I just shrugged it off. I had in my short time in prison seen worse. Eventually I was given some hot water for my flask and it tasted very sharp and funny. I was told later that the water had lots of dissolved lime in it and this clogged everything up. The food was awful, even worse than in Shotts prison and I thought that was terrible; in my opinion it was so bad that even a hungry dog could not have eaten it. I was glad I was leaving after only one night. The prison bus made four stops to pick up other prisoners, and then we continued the journey south to Durham prison, the first prison over the Scottish border. The journey was uncomfortably long; I was stuck in a very small space perched on a rock hard plastic seat. Our food ration for the day was two sandwiches and a packet of crisps. Arriving at Durham we waited for six hours before being given some supper then we were billeted in C Hall; I had to share the smallest cell I have ever seen, and with a smack head, who was crying because he was in for a mere three days. As I was becoming hardened to others expressing any emotion, beginning to see it as a weakness, I looked at him with total disdain and contempt. I still had a year and a half to go. The night was uneventful, but I was awake most of the night, so I was exhausted the next morning; however I knew that I could sleep in the van as we journeyed south. After I was given breakfast I was glad to be rid of the junkie; his feet stank; in fact his entire body stank. He smelled like he had never stepped in a shower, despite my sarcasm on the smell of the room. His hair and skin were greasy. I know it was the drugs that had made him like this, but sometimes my own pain of being incarcerated and the constant tension made me less than tolerant. So I hated him, I saw this junkie as all that was wrong inside, and on the outside, and my hate was focussed on him. I actually had to stop myself attacking him. My jail head was driving me insane.

On arrival I had asked if I could have a single cell. I was told at 9 o'clock that night that it would be fine. Just as I was settling in for the night, the door opened and this really dirty unwashed guy strolled in, shaking from not having had a hit all day. I went down the stairs to the Guard on duty, and said that the other guy on duty had told me I would remain on my own for the evening. He was very cheeky. I told him that if the guy they had put in my cell irritated me, I would smother him to death. The thing is I knew how unpredictable people with a habit could be going cold turkey, and I just did not want to listen to him withdrawing all night. I wanted peace and quiet. So my threat had some weight, and I think my demeanour alerted them to how much this issue had shaken me.

The next morning I was awoken by three massive prison officers and told to get dressed and taken downstairs. I was threatened with a kicking if I didn't keep quiet. I told the officer that was doing most of the shouting to fuck off, that he was an insignificant little insect that gets off on hurting people because he was bullied at school, or battered about by his wife. He naturally became angry. I replied "that's it, isn't it, your wife beats you up you sad cunt, and you get locked in a cupboard with a plastic hood on and a ball in your mouth while your wife fucks all the neighbours." I was having fun actually, and my jail head meant that I just did not care, because the system had helped make me like this. I was dragged up the stairs and threatened that if I ever talked to an officer like that again I would never walk again without crutches. I was becoming just like every other long term prisoner, I had become like they had made me, in their own image. I was a bully, and I was merely repeating all that I had seen them do, and all that happened to me had made me like this. Due to some administrative error, I was told that I would be here for the time being. I was not pleased at hearing this news. However after calming down, I was allowed to share with a cheeky guy from Liverpool, who shared my sense of humour. Out of the cell window, I could see where Mary West was held; I was also told about a female prisoner who killed her husband, chopped him into little pieces, and made a curry which she fed to his family; interesting, but creepy.

I met a few good blokes there. I was there for nearly a month despite my daily protest asking to be moved. I was told that the transport was cancelled due to not having enough drivers, a common occurrence. I believe this was due to the low wages, and constant bad press making taking this job was something that only the most desperate, and hence the most unreliable would take. This only added to the poor service this privatised situation had caused to the former services. Group 4 security had the contract for prisoner transportation in England whereas Reliance had the contract for Scotland. Reliance is the cheaper service, and as such had to pay their staff less. This resulted in workers with no attachment to their work, and no loyalty either. Eventually the situation resolved and I was on my way once more.

I was next taken to a semi open prison but kept in the cages at the rear. Inside the outer security wall of the prison, there were sections where the prisoners could walk around freely, which was a novelty at first. After this walk like a normal person, we were then put into a secure wing just like the one in the prison I had been in before. This secure wing within the semi open prison was designed like an American prison with sliding barred gates between the 'open' and the secured wings. Inside the secure sections all the cells had steel doors which were never locked. For the first time in a few years, I managed to start getting a full night's sleep without some other prisoner snoring or farting all night, or having to endure the stench of their unwashed feet. I was in the ground floor that used to be a dungeon. It was an easy night after Durham Prison where I had spent a month. I was sharing a cell with a guy that didn't snore; so in many ways it was heaven. I was able to have a peaceful relaxing and refreshing sleep. I remember this so clearly because due to constant sleep deprivation and stress, this was such a rare pleasure. An absolute treat! While it was still prison, the semi open did have a different feel to it. Intimidation was still happening, prison officers were still humiliating convicts and other prisoners were still battling out their own petty little wars, but it was still a little closer to freedom, a little closer to getting out, and a little closer to the end of my time inside.

The next morning I was taken to Winchester prison. The prison was built with a central hub shaped like a light house, which had five parts making it look like a cycle wheel I imagine from the air. Its design was very much based on the original design by the 'utilitarian' Jeremy Bentham and his 'panopticon' where all prisoners were constantly under surveillance. Even when prisoners were not being directly observed, the architecture itself was 'controlling' and influencing behaviour as there was always the possibility that someone was watching, just like 'big brother' in the film 1984. Winchester wasn't a very large prison. It had a capacity of around 700. All were category B prisoners; there were no 'category A' prisoners in this prison as it was a semi open. I was told that this place was full of sex offenders, rapists, and child molesters; however while they were a danger on the outside, they were not considered dangerous to other prisoners. I was billeted in the main wing on the third floor of B Hall.

I was let out for recreation on my first night there before lock up. I had a game of pool then had a seat. This guy sat down next to me and started chatting, saying that this prison wasn't too bad. I asked him what he was in for; his reply was 'a very bad thing'. I asked him what he meant, and then he said he had raped his cousin. I suddenly stood up and walked to the far end of the room and asked someone if he was right in the head. The prisoners said that they were all mixed now down south and that if they said anything to these particular prisoners, they would be punished and taken to the segregation wing. Personally I would rather have gone to the segregation wing than mix with them. I didn't know who I was talking to most of the time. I guess we all want to know who we are talking to, and if we can trust them. Inside prison, the usual rules do not apply. At dinner I would hear stories and they disturbed me. Often there was some gossip about someone murdering kids, burying them in pieces after cutting their bodies up, or of burning them. One inmate was rumoured to have kept one of his victims in the chest freezer at a low enough temperature, but not frozen, so he could molest the body whenever he wanted. I just could not listen to these stories for too long as I had enough to think about most of the time.

After breakfast, I was off in the morning to Parkhurst prison, which I was told wasn't too bad. It had a dreadful reputation but I had become used to the madness and insanity of prison life and did not think that it could be any worse than any other prison I had seen, and anyway I was only going to be there for a month. The prison is located on the Isle of Wight and we were heading for Newport. We took a long route, as usual, as we had to pick up two more prisoners on the journey. By the time we arrived at the ferry port in Southampton we had been travelling for six hours. In the real world a journey that would take no more than half an hour.

The ferry journey was uncomfortable as we had to stay in the van. If anything had happened we were going down with the ship with the Captain. . We could feel the constant struggle, as the current threatened to push and pull this ferry off course. I lost myself in the sound of the whine of the engines as they struggled to find purchase against the strong current of the Solent.

When we arrived at the Isle of Wight, as we travelled along the costal roads, the waves were hitting the van as it drove along heading for the prison. I could see them from the side window. I was on the left side of the van near the front. It was wonderful and exciting to see the power of the waves, and smell the salt of the sea. We were huddled together in this van in small locked boxes inside a locked van to which only the officers had a key. At this time you have nothing but your imagination and self doubt to contend with in all situations. I remember this being one time when I felt powerless to alter anything that could have happened. Had we been blown over the wall by a large wave we would have drowned for sure. Despite a long wait in the van, we eventually arrived safely in one piece. As usual, on arrival we needed to wait at reception before we could be allowed inside the prison.

We were billeted in the old hospital wing where Reggie Kray resided. This place was really old.

On arrival I was told that we had to stay there for a week for a full prison induction. When I and another guy I had come to know in Winchester asked about purchasing something from the prison canteen we were told we couldn't have anything to eat as we had no money. As my family always made sure I had money, I knew this had to be a mistake. I had some money in Durham and that was the link to the transfer from the English system from the Scottish one. After a full day of going into the prison officers office on the ground floor he gave us £10 pound each to buy some food and other essentials until he had the paperwork sorted and the money would be taken off once the paperwork and bank system had been notified. This was just another typical process of the way every prison system works.

The doors and floors were made of wood unlike the steel ones that characterises just about every other prison I had seen; the floor sprung when you walked on it, reminding me of a school gym hall. In each cell, the wooden door had a flip down lid half the size of the door. When the prison officer came round on his check I nearly shit myself when I saw a full head and shoulders come through the door.

We were let out our cells for a good part of the day. It was laid back and there was not a lot of tension as Parkhurst only held around forty prisoners with most of them on remand. I liked it. There was an area at the back of the prison hospital; it was like a small garden with flowers and a small rockery with the highest fence I had ever seen. One of the prison officers who seemed to me to be a bit more human than some of the others told us it was where the Kray twins and Peter Sutcliff used to walk around. This prison was small in comparison to some of the others I had been in. It had one floor above the ground level. The first floor, where I was being held, had an area at the end of the left hand section that led to a hall. It looked like a classroom.

On the ground floor there was a pool table, two wall phones, and a set of stairs that led to the hospital wing. The prison office was also on the ground floor and at the top of the stairs was the office of the prison doctor. It was weird being here as I had read the book 'The Krays' written by Philip Ridley adapted into a film, starring the Kemp brothers. After I had become used to the excitement of being in the same prison that had housed the famous Kray twins, life here became just like any other prison, with boredom, intimidation, and everything requiring a decision wrapped in red tape. A week passed without any incident, and I was moved to B hall.

The main building in Parkhurst prison had five landings with two single cells on each wing, meaning that all of the other cells were for shared occupancy. This was not too bad as this time I was again sharing with the guy from Liverpool I had met in Durham. He was short, heavy but not fat, with close cropped ginger hair, and thin set eyes. I had to say that at first glance he looked kind of hard and had been a prisoner long enough to perfect the 'don't stare at me or there will be trouble' look about him. But despite him being a good lad and all, I still wanted my privacy, my own space which I had become used to.

The next morning I asked to talk to a supervisor and explained the fact that I was an enhanced prisoner in Scotland and I should be put in an enhanced wing while I was in this English prison. A call was made to my personal officer who looked after all paperwork for a small group of prisoners and I was moved to C wing on the other side of the prison. Negotiating my rights in prison was the toughest part of the sentence, but to be honest everywhere was the same; it was how you handled it. C wing had only single cells, and I settled in and had a wander around. There were cookers, fridges and the canteen sheet listed creatine powder, which was good as I had been training hard, and wanted to improve my muscle tone, protein powder to keep my weight down, and there were even beef, chicken, and cheese salads and sweets including chocolate. I could even buy a budgie like the bird man of Alcatraz if I had wanted; there were all kinds of vegetables, rice, pet food for budgies, and hamster pellets. Compared to Scotland, this was just like a supermarket!

While the conditions were more human in terms of the food, and other luxuries, it was fairly difficult to go to the gym; they did try to make the system fair, where odd numbered cells went on one day, and the even numbers attended on another day, but it was still difficult for me to become part of the routine here as I was only to be there for such a short time. As it turned out I was there for 3 weeks, and as a result I needed something to do so I asked if I could go to an education class or join a work party. All work parties were full but I was told I could join an existing education class.

I was given a place in one in the Arts and Crafts department at the bottom end of the prison with a view of the ocean, such a simple pleasure, and something I had not seen since being stuck in the van on my journey to the Isle of Wight, but that had been terrifying to be honest. It was great to see calm ocean water again. The simple pleasures are the most satisfying ones when deprived of your freedom. When you're out, you take so much for granted. Inside prison, you do miss the smallest of things.

I was there in the class every morning and in the afternoon after lunch. I made a few things in the arts classes. I wasn't allowed to take them with me as it would have taken too long to complete the correct paperwork. So I donated the drawings and craftwork to other prisoners. The 'red tape' paperwork and bureaucracy was just a nightmare and just not worth the hassle. I made a clay eagle and a depiction of Jesus on a cross which I left for two of the guys I was inside with. It kept me busy, and I enjoyed the creative side it brought out in me.

I remember one particular prisoner who had just completed his 22nd year inside. I was intrigued and asked him the reason for the length of his sentence. He mentioned that he was in for murder, and that he was innocent of killing his wife and would not admit he was guilty to the parole board, so as he would not admit his guilt, his sentence was to be fully served. Just like in the film 'The Shawshank Redemption' everyone inside prison was innocent. In Parkhurst I was told that my girlfriend could come and visit me. I had longed for female company, and the soft touch of a woman, and it was great to see her, smell her perfume, and hear her laugh. It was such a pleasure that I did try and stay there in Parkhurst, as it was easier for her to visit. I contacted the Home Office but didn't get anywhere. I was told by the prison officers that it was all politics and costs and that's why I wouldn't get a transfer, I was returning to Scotland. The rejection hit me hard, and everything annoyed me more than usual. There was a guy in the next cell that played the track "I'm so lonely" on repeat, and it was so annoying that it was driving me insane. I approached him calmly at first and I asked if he wanted to borrow some CDs as I was tired of listening to the same song every day. He took my request as a threat and he ran down the stairs and shouted to the prison officers that I was being racist, this shocked me; perhaps he didn't like Jocks? It was the fact that he was around eighteen stones of muscle that I found hard to understand why he thought I was provoking him. I did get into a lot of bother because of that incident; as I was to find out; I wasn't accepted by most of the English there. I got on well with two Scots guys there though and a few of the Russians that were inside for kidnapping. They told me how they only took their own kind, Russian people with cash, and they would send body parts to the families if they didn't pay up. I imagined myself as a Russian gangster for a few seconds and demanding cash with menaces seemed quite sexy for a second; then I realised hey, everyone in prison was caught doing some sort of crime so nothing is without risk.

I had been at Parkhurst for around three weeks when I was told I was leaving in the morning. I was furious, all that way for three weeks, and just one visit from my girlfriend! I had just come down with some sort of stomach bug and felt totally awful during this time. When it was time to start travelling, telling the officers that I was too ill to leave did not go down too well at all. I lost a lot of weight travelling, as I just could not face food at all. The next morning after being told I was moving again took the exact same route back to Scotland and yes, it took another month. By the time both trips had finished, I had lost over two stones and was looking dreadful. Eventually I arrived back at Shotts prison and was well enough to get back into the gym. My first training session didn't go as planned as a fight broke out. One of the guys hit another in the face with a fifteen-kilo weight. I also overheard a prisoner slagging me off, but I waited until the right time to retaliate. I wanted to humiliate him in front of all his mates. That night, during supper, I confronted him and had it out with him, I only managed one punch when the inevitable fight broke out, during which he ran away so fast he left his slippers on the stairs. The next day an officer informed me that I was on a charge for hitting someone. So in protest that night I tore the cell apart. All the shelves, cupboard doors, sink, everything I could destroy, I put out the window. Inevitably I was taken to segregation. While I have always had the capacity for violence if I had to defend myself, this person that I had become was frightening. I just couldn't figure out what the hell was wrong with me. I know now I was suffering depression and frustration. I was angry and couldn't control my emotions, I couldn't calm down, and the only emotions I was now capable of expressing were fear which was now expressed only as rage and anger. In the segregation unit, I was put in a cell that was furnished with a cardboard seat and table and a plastic mattress. But I knuckled down like the pro I had become and just did my time, waiting, always waiting on something happening to break the monotony.

In a controlled environment like prison, and especially a segregated unit within a prison, common sense would tell you that it would be harder for contraband and illicit goods to be brought in, but this was just not the case. The passing of drugs was a common occurrence in the segregated unit. Every time I settled down, I was asked by someone in another cell to pass something over to someone else. I did it, I had no choice really. I had realised that it was easier to take part in the system than to fight it, and apart from helping contraband find its way from cell to cell, there was nothing else to do besides sleeping and reading which had started to make me feel tired. One route of passing something was by using a newspaper. The technique was to put the goods between two pages and seal it with toothpaste and this would be passed under the door. It was never detected. The windows had gaps that a hand could fit through and, if you squeezed hard enough, even your whole arm. When a weight such as an orange or other heavy fruit was attached to a bed cover that had been pleated together into a rope, this makeshift pendulum could be swung from one cell window to another. This did pass the dreary days, and sometimes making these things, and planning how to help others passed the time quite quickly. The only down side of being in segregation unit was I had no personal possessions. I did not have my guitar or anything that helped pass time; these things were not allowed as they could potentially be used as a weapon. While inside the unit, I was told I would be sent to Edinburgh Prison a week later. I liked that idea as I had been there when I was being transferred to the south and it had a full time education programme. This meant that I could finish my English Higher and then take a computer skills class.

One of the guys in the next cell told me about a fight he was involved in over a simple mispronounced word. He was talking to another prisoner who apparently said something in jest and he battered him near to death, which is why he was put into the segregation unit. It's hard to explain to people just how frustrating it all is, and how easy these little things become massive. It's true there are some really annoying people everywhere you go, but on the outside you can just walk away or stop associating with them. Inside you just can't get away from them. Since the start of this nightmare that was the bulk of my time in the segregation unit, I had not slept a full night without wakening up feeling some regret about all the wrongs I had done in my life and putting my head in my hands and feeling like shit. That's what prison had made me, an insomniac, with nothing but time to reflect on all of the things that most people can keep busy to forget. Despite waking up in a cold sweat most nights, the week passed quickly and I was transferred to Edinburgh.

Chapter 17

SAUGHTON PRISON EDINBURGH

By now I was something of a prison expert, having travelled and stayed in so many I knew I would be hosed down with cold water in the induction wing. As was usual, prisoners had to share cells until they were processed and allowed to become part of the main prison. The guy I shared with in these first few days was ok and he didn't snore. After three days of induction, I put my name on the list for full time education programme and I was told a few days later that I had been successful. This surprised me, as many times I had been disappointed. Edinburgh was a working prison; everyone needed to do something to keep busy. Most prisoners wanted to work in the gardens where all the opportunities were as prisoners had the chance to bring something in, and make some easy money. I was soon moved to the semi open part of the prison and right away applied and completed the paperwork to be moved to an open prison, but as I had been in so much trouble, I would have to wait for three months before I would be considered for an open prison.

There was tension in Edinburgh but not as much as in a closed prison because everyone wanted to move to a more relaxed open prison. So violence was rare and petty personal vendettas so common in 'normal' prison regimes were kept to a minimum. This general relaxation also helped the prisoners to have more liberties than would normally be allowed in a tightly controlled closed prison, as you could get away with a lot more there. It wasn't too bad; the main gates were closed at night and our cell doors were open all night so I could wander around the hallway in the section and had the opportunity to make some toast or use the communal microwave. Some of the prisoners were allowed out, sometimes for days or even weeks to prepare them for their release; some even had day jobs on the outside to prepare them for the open prison regime. Some of the lifers too could have this privilege. There was a lot of contraband brought in due to that freedom. Home visits for a few hours could be set up and there wasn't much of a search by the prison officers who certainly wanted to keep the atmosphere relaxed; however they did still do their job and some searches resulted in confiscation of say a mobile phone or drugs or alcohol, although with a little ingenuity and imagination, people were still able to smuggle in just about anything. Once you get used to that small freedom and perk, the boredom set in and we would wish our lives away looking out the window, longing for real freedom, the independence to just decide when and what to do, outside in the world, outside of the prison. I remember looking out one sunny day; I could see people in the distance having a barbecue; this was heart wrenching for me. I wanted to be the person with a beer in one hand and a chicken drumstick in the other, while talking to ordinary people. I imagined I could smell the sweet pungent aroma of barbecue cooked chicken, the bitter sweet cool tang of an ice cold beer, and the warmth and sensuality of a woman close to me. Damn I thought as my mind came crashing back to reality, why was I inside? Why did I have to wait so long for a taste of freedom? As I felt the surge of hope rise within me, I smiled at my naivety for allowing myself the selfish indulgence of feeling anything other than anger, and fear, the only emotions that helped me survive in the harsh reality of life inside a prison. The semi open was less tough than the high security prisons, and time was passing by. Every day I would check with the guards to find out the status of my application for the open prison. Eventually after what seemed like an age, I was informed that I would be moving north from Edinburgh to an open prison. I was offered a place in an open prison called Castle Huntley, near Dundee. I jumped at the chance even though I had been told that it was also overcrowded. Although I wanted to move as soon as was possible, everything in prison takes time. I was messed around for a while with a check into my background. This is carried out by the social worker to find out if a prisoner has any problems in the location they are being transferred to. I asked my lawyer to look into this and try to speed up the process, and he eventually informed me that I would be moving a month later.

Chapter 18

THE OPEN PRISON SYSTEM

I was escorted from my cell and taken to reception where I collected my belongings and waited for the van to pick me up. When it arrived I was surprised to see that it was a small prison escort van. I had expected to be handcuffed inside a cell in the van. I realised that as I was travelling to an open prison, this was a signal, a sign that things would now be different. There was a driver and a private security officer in the back with us. However when the back of the small van was opened imagine my surprise when there were small cell inside this too, with the usual long chain which would secure all prisoners to the cells inside the van. Sitting in the van I started thinking of the time I had already spent and the people that I had received letters from. I had letters every day in my first few months inside then became fewer and after a while, I was only receiving correspondence from my close family, my sister and my two brothers, and my daughter. Letters are so important to prisoners, as they are a window through your imagination to the outside, to freedom, and just to make sense of the madness of prison. Reading a letter allows you for a brief moment to be set free from the confines of the prison walls. Reading about events, stories, and even the mundane things people did allowed me in the privacy of my cell when alone to be free as I read. So these things were very important, and anyone who did not receive anything from anyone was even more of a prisoner, and was punished even more by the pain of confinement. That's when you know who you can really and truly count on, when someone takes the time to connect to you.

On the way to the open prison we had a detour to Shotts to pick up more prisoners. It was not too awful, and by now I knew the procedure and just let it all wash over me; I knew a few of them from Barlinnie where I had been placed on remand awaiting my sentence. I had some catching up to do as I hadn't seen them for almost two years. As we caught up with our gossip, the distance was rendered meaningless; as was the passage of time, and before we knew it we had arrived at the 'Castle'. We were told we could have whatever we wanted from the belongings the prison system had taken form us when we were first admitted to jail. This was great as I hadn't seen some of my personal belongings since I had started my sentence over two years before. But the novelty wore off as soon as we arrived at the open prison and saw the conditions. There were five people to a single room; there was a TV in the dormitory but there was always an argument about what programme should be on, or who was using it for a DVD or a game. All through my sentence I had found myself slipping slowly into a routine that I was in bed by 11pm, and would usually be asleep at 11.30 every night. So you can imagine that when one of the guys I was sharing a room with wanted to watch TV until two or three in the morning, it soon caused arguments and stress. I started to wear ear plugs to gain a little oasis of calm in the madness that was freedom in a semi open prison.

Although mobile phones are not allowed, almost everyone had one. You could get one easy for a few pounds. There was so much contraband coming in; it was hard to believe I was still in prison. It was more like a supermarket! I saw drugs, phones, and steroids, anything you wanted you could get, for a price. The part of the prison I was living always smelt of burning heroin, a dry acrid nauseating smell that I could never ever get used to. I guess with the general disrepair and poor environment many of the junkies felt totally at home. This prison was damp, with plaster board falling from the ceiling. The upside to the relaxed atmosphere was that we could wander over some of the grounds until 9 o'clock in the evening. As I hadn't been out in the dark for a long time, it was such a pleasure to walk among grass and trees, and see the night sky, and smell the cold fresh northern Scottish air in my nostrils. It's amazing how small things mean a lot to us and we take them for granted every day. It was hard to get used to this sort of environment and settle in after the brutality of a closed prison.

Two prisoners I had become friends with, Jimmy, Dan and I would sit on a bench next to a 5 aside football area at the back of the prison and look up at the open sky. Just to be outside talking shit and smiling was a pleasure, a joy, and to feel that free was a gift. We wanted freedom and the little things in life that had been denied us. However even in this much relaxed environment, I still needed to watch my back though; it's more dangerous because prisoners with a grudge and a score to settle have a bit more freedom with blind spots from which they can attack their prey. So I never lost my jail head, even in this relaxed atmosphere.

I applied and completed the paperwork for family to visit me. The day came that I could see them; I was so excited to meet them outside prison walls. I could hardly contain myself. I walked up to the visiting area and waited. The place is so hard to find and so far for them to travel that they did get lost; their time was also taken up because they had brought me a hamburger meal from the local MacDonald's. I met them at their car; it was so great to see them. We ate our food sitting at a table in a large picnic area next to the visiting area. Wow did that feel good to just walk around with them and hug freely without anyone getting rugby tackled to the ground suspected of passing drugs. In other prisons the prison officers were so suspicious they trusted no one. I felt excited; I could say what I wanted without lip readers watching us but I didn't know what to say. It would take time to adjust to this as the harsh environment of a closed prison cannot fully prepare anyone for even the smallest of freedoms, and the feelings I was experiencing were overwhelming me. This was like another world for me, like I wasn't there. I had become so used to being told when to eat, when to exercise, when to get up and walking in single file everywhere that this kind of freedom, even though restricted in ways, was still not real yet. I kept waiting for someone to put me in a cell for just walking in the corridors.

Chapter 19

SURVEILLANCE – HERE'S LOOKING AT YOU KID!

In the full secure prisons the prison guards observe your every move on camera; professional lip readers are also employed. Attempting to stop drugs entering prison is taken seriously. Their focus or targets are dealers or prisoners with known drug problems. However it does not stop it. What does happen is perhaps not intended. The camera will pass all prisoners from time to time and often they do interpret innocent things as potentially criminal. If you have been the focus of their attention, when the visit is over, you can be taken behind a locked door, where you will be asked questions, and then stripped searched if the answers are not satisfactory for them.

In the visiting rooms, there are many prison officers all against the walls, all watching everyone for signs of anything being passed from visitor to prisoner or vice versa. During one of the first visits my family made to see me in Glenochil, I made a simple mistake and did not sit on the right chair, the red one, the one that the camera could easily focus on. I had incorrectly sat on a black one, intended for the visitors, and this simple mistake had ensured that I would be strip searched. I had broken the rules, and I was punished for it. I did not do that again. It is a very tense time, and in high security prisons, one wrong word and the visit could be immediately terminated without any explanation, which I did see from time to time. All visitors were searched before the visit, and everyone was watched throughout a visit, so there was not always a focus on drugs addicts, or their partners. Occasionally a couple who had not seen each other were clearly trying to have some sort of sexual contact, and this was difficult to watch, as it was just so desperate, and embarrassing for everyone concerned.

Occasionally the guards would stop them; usually they would just watch them. During some of my visits with my family it was difficult trying to have a conversation anyway, as it was strained with me trying to let them know I was ok, so as not to worry them, but at the same time realising that this was just so unnatural, to try to have normal conversation when people were watching your every move, and potentially 'hearing' or reading your every word. And desperate couples were necking and masturbating each other just a few feet away. This was not at all comfortable.

Every prison had slightly different ways of putting inmates under surveillance, they all had different rules but all were very strict. If a prisoner was spotted doing something considered against the rules then they were rugby tackled to the ground by three prison officers. However sometimes prisoners were stopped after the visit and could be subjected to a strip search. On some occasions prisoners were stopped at random, and that happened to me many times. Often I was pulled out of the line took aside taken to a side room and stripped naked, whereby an officer would then shine a torch up my arse, and then I would be told to dress and be sent on my way. As I was not using drugs, and I was not part of any criminal network inside, I was angry at these invasions of my privacy at first. And although I knew I had nothing to hide, I do remember that I still felt guilty; the look they give you to justify what they were doing implied that at some point their searches would reveal that I was hiding something. Although this was at first humiliating it was an everyday occurrence in prison. During a search they ask you to stand with your legs apart, bend over and open your anus for them to shine their little torch, and then you are asked to turn around and lift up your balls, and then to pull back your foreskin. At first bending over opening yourself to them is bloody terrible then after this horror becomes routine, you start doing it automatically before they even ask.

I usually tried to cooperate as my main goal was always to get to Noranside Prison, an open prison that allowed inmates much more freedom than the semi open prison called Castle Huntley. I had heard many good things from other prisoners all the way through my sentence so my mind was set, and I was determined to get there. I wanted to get a transfer to Noranside and work in the forestry department and work towards some qualifications in the form of certificates. I put in a form for a transfer and kept a check on it to see how it was proceeding. Like everything else in the prison service, it takes a long time to get things sorted. I also had to arrange home visits as Edinburgh had done nothing to forward my background check and it was coming up for Christmas. I wanted out; even to a hostel or homeless unit would have satisfied me. I wanted to talk to other people outside the system as you find whatever you have in common with a person who is inside with you, that's mostly what is talked about, your time inside, what you've done, and what's going on inside. For instance if you were a member of a gym or sport that's what you would talk about there, it's the same inside. We would talk about our previous life, family, friends, what you have done and achieved but it's mostly where you are within the prison sentencing levels and how long you have left or if you have a home leave that is usually discussed. I had a personal officer who was working hard to get me to Noranside but at the time it was like an overcrowded night club, with the doormen saying, 'one in, and one out'. However, a few days later, I received the good news that I was to leave the next day for the open prison. Well, on hearing this, I was packed within an hour and the long night ahead passed quickly, but I slept only occasionally as I was both excited and scared at the changes ahead. I knew it was a lot stricter in the open regime but that's what I wanted. I wanted discipline; that's what I had become used to; this shows you what I had become, so even getting to the open prison changes nothing after what they do to you in the closed prisons. In the morning I was the first one at the reception ready to go. I put my bags on the stagecoach bus storage on the side of the bus. I walked round to the front of the bus, and felt ordinary, normal, not like a prisoner. I was like a teenager on his first date; it was heaven, all of this freedom! I stood outside and had a cigarette. I met the other three guys that were going to Noranside. When we stepped on the bus, it was like travelling in a limousine after the prison bus journeys I had experienced. We were not handcuffed, and we could talk and joke or sleep or do anything we wanted on the bus just like normal people. This was going to be interesting, I thought.

Chapter 20

NORANSIDE OPEN PRISON

It only took around half an hour to get to Noranside Prison from Castle Huntley. It looked impressive; it was a hospital at one time for people who suffered from breathing problems. That's why it was so far from the towns and cities and why it had the reputation of having fresh unpolluted air. There was a small farm at the entrance to the prison. After we had arrived an officer led us without chains or handcuffs to where our cells were. After dumping my bags on the bed, Sid, one of the guys I had befriended at the castle gave me a guided tour round the prison. It was November and as were so far north the snow was around five inches deep. It was an awesome sight, all that countryside covered in a blanket of pure white snow. It felt just like Christmas, and that I was staying at a country lodge, rather than being in a prison. There were two separate houses at the top end of the prison grounds away from the main billeting wings. These houses were used to reintegrate and prepare prisoners close to the end of their sentence learn skills required to help them cope, and prevent recidivism. So anyone in these private, unsupervised houses were also considered to be the types that needed further help with cooking, budgeting and just normal skills required to survive outside prison. I wanted to be up there as soon as I saw it, away from what could potentially get me into trouble and sent back to a closed prison. I knew that as all your troubles tend to follow you in prison, potential rivalries, petty squabbles, and perceived slights could all potentially get me sent back to a closed high security prison. I had already met one of the guys that I had punched in Shotts prison; however he only lasted a week in the open prison as he was far too paranoid to cope with all the open space, and few places to hide. I was told he had put an old woman in a coma with a claw hammer to steal her pension book, which he sold to buy drugs. In prison there are no secrets, eventually everyone finds out everything about you, either from the staff, or from the other prisoners.

I remember the morning of my first day in Noranside. It was great; we were let out of the sections at eight o'clock in the morning and one of my friends called Harry came to my room and showed me where to go to get breakfast. It was quite a large area, with six tables on the right side of the room and four on the other. On entering the dining room, just inside the door was the cook's area; it was set up like a bakers shop with everything on offer to eat on display. This was such a joy, and meant that I could actually eat in a prison again, something that I had been avoiding for ages. I also found to my excitement that it had one of those moving grills that you find in hotels and guesthouses, where your bread is toasted by a conveyer belt that moves the bread under the heating elements. There was even orange juice! After breakfast we went to the farm to have a look around then to the work parties and to the garden centre where they sold garden benches, green houses, garden huts and plants that the prisoners had made or grown. This place was interesting to me, and was not like anything I had seen before. It was still a prison, but the surveillance was very low key, and based on trust, rather than punishment to keep order. Compared to the high security prison, this was so different.

We had a look around the gym and the education centre. I immediately applied for Art, English and Computing classes; then I registered with the forestry vocational training classes so I could have some certificates which could help me find work if I stayed in Scotland on my release. So I was set for the rest of my time left in prison. All I needed to do was keep my head down and get on with it. I met a prisoner called Rick. He was a bit of a head case, not in the violent sense but funny. There were animals all around the prison, like rabbits, hares, and on occasions I even saw deer. Ricky was lonely and said he needed a pet, so he captured a rabbit which he discovered one night on a walk outside. When I went to his room to ask him if he wanted to go for a walk, to my amazement he had this rabbit in his room. We convinced him to let it go, that he wasn't allowed to keep it. Another time when we went out for a walk in six inches of snow, Ricky didn't come out with us saying he had a visit. We were about half way down the road and heard this loud scary grunting sound coming from a dark hunched up figure on all fours. It came running out, roaring and snorting. We were all amazed to see this wild pig just heading straight for us. Harry ran away down part of the road, PJ jumped out the way and Tommy fell on the snow trying to run away. I just froze. We heard loud laughing and Ricky stood up and came to the light grinning, he had been the source of all the bleating and snorting! I told him I thought he was a wild pig. Harry thought it was a wolf. He laughed again and said 'We are in the wrong country, you idiots!". We never heard the end of that one.

That weekend, Ricky was due a visit and told us he was getting some alcohol dropped off by his visitors in the grounds, and that we could help him collect it after the visiting period was over. The difficulty was to smuggle it in the building as there were random spot checks and patrols and the prison officers did use binoculars to spy on the prisoners on occasions. After the visit at around eight o'clock, an hour before lock up, we made our way out the back of the prison. We sneaked past the prison officers who were watching TV in their small office. I was the lookout while the other two picked up a bottle of vodka and a bottle of Southern Comfort. We didn't want to take it in and get caught so we tried to slip it in the bathroom window in the middle of B section. The window only opened a few inches and the ledge was hard to reach. Ricky levered the bottle down and tried to drop it on the ledge and it smashed. We ran like maniacs into Ricky's cell and just tried to look innocent. The whole section was stinking of alcohol; it was funny but very risky at the same time. He did however manage to get the vodka in by asking someone to bring in. I didn't drink any of it. I didn't want it or need it and didn't want a hangover as the gym was the one thing that kept me fit, sane and on the wagon. Anyway I had done enough of that before I went in and sickened myself with it. But it had been so exciting to take part in such a risky adventure. It was like school camp that night!

After a period in the induction wing a large billeting hall with lots of beds in tidy rows, I applied for a single cell in C wing. The system of drug testing in this open prison was more severe with harsher penalties. If someone was discovered to have used drugs they were immediately sent back to a high security prison; this meant that many prisoners who tested positive created space for other clean prisoners who did not use drugs. Much to my delight I was moved within weeks, I now had my own cell.

I didn't get the Christmas home leave I had applied and hoped for; my paperwork had not been completed properly. I later redid this, but I was so upbeat by this time and I was getting used to this sort of inefficiency. Nothing was done to anyone in this system without everything being checked and checked again. All of these rules and regulations were baffling and unnecessary, but while I agreed with many, I believe that most were in place with the intention to frustrate and punish the prisoners that officers did not like. It was common for paperwork to go missing, or lack an essential signature, and remain locked in the administration system if someone had upset an officer. This constant process of waiting for paperwork to be completed, to be passed up or down the chain of command was frustrating and one of the hardest things to deal with once you were used to the routine violence and constant atmosphere of intimidation in prison. It was really mind numbing and this is one of the main reasons people inside were on edge. Months of built up frustration of waiting for something, whether it was a visit or a move, or for a piece of clothing or footwear from the outside. When a decision was made which was not in your favour, you needed to find another approach and start the process all over again. So British, a beautiful, wasteful system, in fact just like your local council. How to constantly frustrate everyone, while everyone gets a chance to have their say in the chain of command, and no one gets the full blame if something is not done correctly. It's a system for the benefit of the prison officers, and certainly not for the prisoners. It's just like the NHS too; where all the systems in place are not for the benefit of the patients but the protection of the staff, should something go wrong. There were only twelve people in the entire prison over the Christmas week, the place was deserted but it was nice and quiet just the way I preferred it. I passed the time over that week by looking after the animals. There was a small farm at the bottom of the prison with rabbits, gerbils, ferrets, and even guinea pigs. There were lots birds, chickens, geese, and duck. It was great. I had fresh eggs every morning. I loved it even though I was up at six in the morning to feed them, then once more in the afternoon, and finally last thing at night; I could have done that for the rest of my sentence and it would have been a joy, the time would have passed so quickly.

I had settled in without incident. It was good to have a cell to myself again. Not having to share meant that I was not as tightly wound or as pressured as some of the other prisoners who were forced to share their cells with others. In prison all you do is waiting, and ask for permission for some basic freedom to be granted. I think the system is designed for prisoners to feel grateful to the system for its 'fairness' and it's leniency in giving you this privilege. This results in making unstable people into time bombs waiting to go off at the slightest provocation. I watched this happen daily, and even sometimes I was like that myself. It just gets to you, and you need to let off the steam that builds up in this pressure cooker environment that seems designed not just to punish you, but to humiliate you, make you resentful, and full of hate, anger and the desire for retribution and fairness.

Although Noranside is an open prison, prisoners are locked in their wings from nine at night and night shift takes over until the prison sections are opened again in the morning. They patrol every hour although the section is open. There are three main sections, C, D and E. Within these wings, there are smaller sections. These are single cells and there is a waiting list for them. The larger sections were all double cells. It usually takes around a month to be moved to a single cell in C section. Both floors in that section have twenty cells along a very thin corridor with a toilet at the far end. The sections are closed off but you can still walk around the cells as they are left open.

I was billeted in C section on the ground floor and quickly I took stock of the situation. In this prison, like in all others, and like at school and work, there were people who just had to bully others. In most cases they behave like this because they are just as scared and just as insecure as everyone else is. Once I pointed this out to them, they soon left me alone, but it was still hurtful to watch the weak being preyed on by the 'strong'. One person who preyed on the weak was called Freddy, a petty drug dealer who kidnapped and tortured people that couldn't pay their debts.

Finally came the time for me to get a home leave; all my paperwork was complete; my brother had met with social workers and I was due to get three days leave - a long weekend from Friday to Sunday. I was so looking forward to this I just wanted to feel free and not have the feeling that someone was watching my every move. I was worried about what it would be like and whether I should stand up for myself or let things go if I had a confrontation with someone. I wondered whether I should I back down or do what I do inside and go for it. I worried about what I would say if I met anyone who knew me. Should I tell them that I was still a prisoner?

I wanted the visits to go well but I was worried about what to talk with my family and friends as technically I was still a prisoner. Did I have to be careful about telling people my opinions about the prison system? I really didn't want anything coming back to me, and I did not want to be punished or lose my place in the open prison, which I found enjoyable, and which was, despite it being a prison, truly tolerable, and certainly preferable to the harsh regime of the high security prisons I had been in before. As I had not had a normal conversation for a few years I worried about being tongue tied. When I arrived in Glasgow, I wanted to kiss the ground and shout 'I'm free' but I wasn't free; I was on leave. I was worried about drink or drug tests when I returned as if I tested positive for either I would lose my single cell entitlement, and risk the possibility of being sent to a high security prison. I did not take an aspirin, or even a liqueur chocolate for fear of being punished on my return! I also worried about how I would react to women if they spoke to me. Would they know I was just out of prison, would they see the hunger and desperation for affection in my eyes? Before prison I had been able to talk to women easily, but now I really felt uncomfortable just the thought of talking to one again.

Before my home leave Harry and I visited the gym for our nightly workout and he accidentally bumped into a new comer to the prison with an old school attitude. It was left at a mean look from the new comer but later in the kitchen area at the microwave making pasta, the guy walked up behind Harry and said he was going to kill him. Harry didn't want trouble at a crucial point in his sentence but this guy wanted Harry to look weak before walking away, so someone had to back down or a fight would ensue. This was another of many things that happened to nearly everyone in this place and its bloody hard to look cowardly and back off but so easy to lose everything, so Harry had to back down, lose face, or lose his place inside this open prison with its privileges of being allowed out.

I kept my own pressure on the prison officers to get to the houses and was moved to one of the houses which had single cells and held twelve prisoners. There were two sections to each house. I was in the larger of the two. Entering the front door to the left of the corridor was the prison officers office then at the end of the hall was a fire door that led to the outside of the prison grounds.

I was living in a hostel before I was given my prison sentence as I had began drinking, had stopped working and eventually could not pay rent lost my flat. So it was thought that I needed rehabilitated for the outside world. To be honest I had been drinking and was living in a hostel, but I was far from your typical down and out drinking on a street corner. However, I used every edge I had to get up there, and played along with the stereotype of not being able to cope, where I knew I would have a little more freedom, a little more privacy. Inside these houses, specially trained prison officers taught all of the inmates cooking skills, budgeting, and all of the abilities considered necessary for independent living. I just wanted away from the hustle and bustle of the main wings. It was the most comfort I had had in a long while. Each section had a kitchen and instead of going to the dining room in the main prison, a budget of £20 pounds per week allowed the house mates to go shopping in the town and buy what they wanted.

At the weekend we could sunbathe in relative peace. There weren't any other prisoners allowed to enter the house. Sometimes I would cook some food for the guys I knew, and we would take turns doing this. Such simple pleasures, but a freedom I had not had for over two years. However getting into this part of the prison required that the officers believe that I needed lessons in cookery, budgeting and other everyday household tasks that had been routine on the outside for me. So I just told them what they wanted to hear, and I went through the courses like the others remembering to keep my opinions to myself. That said I had been deskilled by prison. I could no longer think for myself, I had become used to have most things decided for me, and had learned to do things within a very rigid routine, which had been ruled by the clock. In these houses, the fact that there were only twelve of us meant that confrontation was at a minimum. There were sex offenders in both houses and although this did cause some friction, we had to keep up the appearance of harmony as any breach of the rules, which included arguments, could result in a prisoner being sent back down the halls or worse back to a high security closed prison. The purpose is to help the people that have no skills in cooking; cleaning, budgeting and preparing them as best they could for the outside. The process included preparing a disclosure paper for potential employers describing what you were in for and that you will not re offend. This environment also allows prisoners to learn how to open a bank account and become just like any other member of society. For many of the prisoners, this was alien to them. They had never learned to cook, clean, open a bank account, or even think about doing anything without first looking for an angle, and trying to find a way to as they saw it 'beat the system'.

To open a bank account you need proof you exist in the first place and I had none, as before I had entered prison, the threat of the sentence, my guilt at having caused a death by dangerous driving, and other issues had made me seek solace in the bottle. I had ended up in a homeless unit, and did not really exist anymore; I had fallen through the cracks as they say. I just waited until the system caught up with who I was and I was then able to be open an account when they eventually found me on their data bases. There were two gardens in the front and back of the large house, which added to the peace and tranquillity of this lovely part of Scotland. In a high security environment, other prisoners casually walked into anyone's cell when they felt like it, this was also an opportunity for thieves and this was something that I had hated. In Noranside I wasn't afraid of getting things stolen but on occasion food did go missing and at times people did come into the house without permission but they didn't last long before they were caught and put out either by us or the prison officers.

The first day of my leave was a Friday. On arriving at my home town I was met by my brothers. We went to our little sister's. She is a great cook and the dining table was full of food and there was plenty to drink. It was a good feeling having all my family around me and having the freedom to talk without waiting for the prison officers to pounce on us for touching, hugging, saying the wrong thing. My sister brought up the time she had visited me when I was In Edinburgh and how it made her feel intimidated and frightened to return to that sort of environment. She had come with my two brothers and we sat at the front of the visiting room next to a cold drinks machine. There must have been drugs passed from a guy's girlfriend after they kissed; three prison officers jumped on him sending him flying off his seat and into my little sister. I was bloody furious as they could have taken him out for a search. In most prisons a glass room with a toilet is used for that specific purpose. I called guards in high security prisons 'agent smiths' as they all had dark glasses, ear pieces and uniforms just like the agents from the film 'The Matrix'; they all looked the same. They also at times reminded me of Arnie's role in the film 'The Terminator' described by the character 'Reece' played by Michael Bien. He said that 'they could not be reasoned with, they could not be bargained with', and just like the terminator in the film, they were ruthless in their pursuit of their prey. I told my sister that I found myself in trouble for having a go at them after that visit and had to see the governor. I was given three days cell confinement for that little outburst.

The home cooked food was so good, I ate my fill and I was ready to burst afterwards. We all sat and caught up on what everyone had been up to. It was so strange that everyone had moved on and I was still the same like, I was on pause. But I was so relaxed, it felt great. They think the home leave prepares you for the outside but the damage prison does to the mind doesn't go away easily. Although you get to mix with crowds of prisoners, it's not the same as the crowds outside. The speed of the world, the noise of traffic or even crossing the road made me feel paranoid and anxious. It was also very hard to hold a conversation with people because all you have done over the last few years is follow a military regime and talk about prison stuff. It didn't feel comfortable doing anything without permission.

I had missed out on a lot of things. My life had stood still and theirs had kept moving on. I missed birthdays; Christmases; New Years; holidays. The next day my brother and I went to the gym as he had bought me a day pass. It was a good feeling being in a clean well stocked gym, to be able to work out, and engage in some honest sweating. Afterwards we met our younger brother and went to our old local to have a few beers and catch up on happier times. That evening we went to an ice hockey match;

it was great to see that. It had been a while since I had been in that sort of environment and at times I felt a little out of place. I felt that everyone knew where I had come from.

All too soon though, my freedom had ended and it was time to go back to prison. I felt that I had only been out a few hours rather than a few days. I arrived in Glasgow Central Station, walked round to Queen Street Station where I met up with some of the other prisoners. When we arrived back at the prison, we were breathalysed and some were pulled and drug tested, some randomly and others because they had drug problems. Everything is recorded in files throughout your sentence; they call it intelligence gathering. You don't know that they are keeping records on you until your cell is searched and you find yourself before the governor but by then it's too late. If a prisoner was found guilty of any rule breach, it meant loss of privileges, cell confinement or time in the segregation unit. Depending on the offence you could have time added or a loss of remission, or a prisoner's category could remain high, which was a punishment in itself.

I kept out of trouble and was to be rewarded by another few days on the outside. I couldn't wait. I was given a three-day leave that was to be taken at my brother's house. I had asked if he could get me some time on my own. So my family arranged for me to stay in a hostel in Glasgow. Prison rules say that the leave should be taken in the address stated in the background reports; I was about to break these rules, so I had to keep it very quiet and try and arrange the leave just by letter. As arrangements for the leave are unorganised and always at last minute, my brother wasn't too happy about the lack of notice of my intention. But this is the system and it moves at its own pace. The leave went well and on return there was talk of having a full week's leave rather than just three days.

In this prison, they had a crazy idea, taken from some management book, called 'bed hopping', similar to a 'hot desk' system in some offices, to maximise space and cut costs. In practice this meant that the cell you were in before the leave might not be the same as the one you were allocated on your return. This set up increases the capacity of prisoners in the prison as for each set of prisoners that return, another will start their home leave and so on. Just like in the Navy crew of a submarine when one shift is on duty while the other sleeps, meaning that the same bunk is occupied by the minimum of two people, and sometimes more. So every prisoner had a box for their belongings and you had to make sure that the cell was clean and return your bedding to the laundry. It seemed to work fairly well.

Home visits are not universally agreed with. Some politicians, newspapers and the public were of the opinion that prison should punish, and the red top newspapers just loved to sensationalise the debate by making the public think that these visits were costly, and that many prisoners absconded. This did happen, but it was extremely rare; however the newspapers made the public think that it happened all the time. During my time in Castle Huntley the issue that had caused much concern was about certain prisoners getting leave back to the area where they had committed their terrible crimes. One prisoner had committed violence on his child by shaking the baby so violently that he had become brain damaged and the mother was furious that he was being allowed outside of prison. The paper reported that she was enraged that this prisoner should have a life; however we were often sure that the reporters made these stories up, after learning from someone inside the prison what was going on, and what could be sensationalised. Another high profile case concerned a serial rapist who was allowed to visit his girlfriend on his home leave. Naturally the newspaper helpfully provided a picture as evidence that he had been in a night club. The condition of visits was that no alcohol or drugs were to be consumed. He of course was tested on his return to the prison.

My next visit was to take place down south, where I had decided to move back to on my release. I was dropped off in Dundee train station. My next stop was London. What a nightmare! I arrived at eight in the morning; I was knocked around like a Ping-Pong ball in the train station escalators in the subway, and then squashed in the tube train before getting another train to Portsmouth then another one to my final destination. All in all the travelling from the north of Scotland to the south of England would cost me two days of freedom travelling. By the time I arrived there I was excited and scared and very paranoid at just how fast life was in London. The noise of the traffic, the huge numbers of people, it was just so hard to get used to.

When I arrived at the hostel they weren't expecting me, and while I was angry at the prison officers for not arranging this, I just let the fact that I was free for now sink in, and let the hostel staff sort it out for me, which of course they eventually did. The next day I arranged a visit with Em'. It was good to see her but I wanted to explore everything, look in shops, talk with old friends rather than hang around as I had been in prison for so long. Sex wasn't more important to me than the freedom in itself. Strange, I know but that's how I was feeling at that time. When it is not a part of your life, it becomes the least important thing; the feeling of warmth from someone, and the closeness are more important than the act.

As usual the week flew in and I was heading back to prison. I arrived in Scotland too late for the pickup as in this part of Scotland the timetables were not rigid like they were in large urban areas. Timetables were guidelines, but were rarely kept to by buses. I called the prison to say I was at the pickup point. I was picked up in a prison van, and I was drug tested, drink tested, searched top to bottom when I arrived at prison.

Eventually it was time for me to consider applying for parole and I had a meeting with someone from the parole board. I was very nervous as I knew they would raise the issue of when I had behaved badly, when I had spent time in segregation cells, and the wrecking of a cell, throwing a TV at a prison officer and a few other things. I personally didn't think I would get parole as my time inside had been eventful. A week later I was asked to attend a meeting at the probation office and told I couldn't get parole as the hostel said they did not have a room for me because they operated a drop in service, which required a spare bed at all times for crisis homeless emergencies. I phoned the hostel to check if there was any room available and was told there wasn't, and so I had to wait a little longer than I had anticipated. I called a few times explaining that I wouldn't get out of prison unless they made a room available for me and informed the parole board. After weeks of calling and writing letters asking if they could please secure a room in order that I could be released into their care, they finally said they would give me a room. My parole started two months later than it should have due to the administration hassles between the prison probation services and the homeless hostel that I needed to be released into in order to get housed in my girlfriends' home town. I was so run down through all this pressure that I started to suffer severe migraines. I had them a lot throughout my sentence because of the daily strain of prison life.

The endless paperwork is a grind. Even something like completing a 'sundries form' to order essential toiletries is hard work. Nothing in the prison system is ever easy. On one occasion, I asked if I could have 'creatine powder' – a protein supplement to help with my weight training; it was passed to the head officer and my request was soundly refused. I then put in a request to the assistant governor; again the answer was no. Then the governor also said no. This all took two months. When I asked for an explanation, I was told that this powder could be used to help addicts give a false negative in mandatory drugs tests as it could help to dilute urine and fool the tests. This is not something I had ever heard about, and thought this was total rubbish, but that was their final word on the matter.

I asked a prisoner afterwards and he explained that how someone passes a drug test involves putting some clean urine, often smuggled in with a drug parcel, under the foreskin and burst the cling film which results in a clear drug test; it saves them flushing their systems by drinking water all night. Usually they stay up all night drinking water and pissing trying to flush the metabolites out of their system. They can do this with heroin but cannabis takes another few days and that's how most of the long term drug users are identified. Any drug user with a foreskin can put a condom full of clean urine under the foreskin and this is then burst at the right moment to fool whoever is supervising them. There would always be a new way of trying to get away with taking drugs. If they have a new test there would be a new way invented of trying to beat it.

A few months into my open prison sentence I applied to take part in a week long venture trust trip. This was an excursion organised and staffed by a charity organisation that been contracted to take prisoners out in the wild for three days of walking and two days of canoeing in the far edges of Scotland's barren land in order to give them back their self esteem, and a sense of achievement. I applied and successfully won a place along with eight other prisoners. After being chosen, we would gather once a week to talk about the trip to plan the food pick up points how to behave, learn how to read maps. So for a couple of weeks before the venture we would go for walks in the freezing cold, wet, wind, snow then talk about it, and we would learn from this, and this really did prepare us for the actual week event. I admit it was exciting to have a purpose. This has become something to look forward to. Inside I knew it wasn't going to change my life but it was something to do it was a way out of getting out of the work party, a way of getting out of prison even if it was hard work to climb hills in terrible weather. In my opinion I only had eight others to put up with instead of hundreds, result! Eventually the time to leave for the week came, and just our luck, it had snowed heavily, 'great' I thought, but at the same time, it was just such an adventure. The night before leaving we all slept in the gym hall and headed out in the morning early so as not to disturb anyone else. When we arrived at our destination by van, the walking started, and despite some preparation it was hard work walking on snow with no path, and using only a map and a compass to guide us. The views were breathtaking and the joy of breathing in fresh air was exhilarating. As there were no prison officers with us on this trip we had to make every decision for ourselves. It was such a horror, to have to decide what to do after having lost these simple privileges years before. It was scary but challenging. It would test me to the limit to keep going at times but we all made it through to our destination which was Eilean Shona, where the author J.M. Barrie wrote 'Alice through the looking glass' made into the film Alice in Wonderland. After arriving here, we then had two days in canoes through rivers which would lead us into the open sea. Canoeing against the tide in the open sea was truly difficult, although it was a great experience. On reflection it wasn't all harmony; there were arguments; we had a few secret heroin users with us, who stayed up all night. It was best to say nothing when they held us back in the mornings, but everything evened out in the end. At times we had to miss a meal to make up lost time but all in all it was a good experience. However it did not give me everything back that prison had taken from me.

I was excited about the parole as the weeks grew closer but I kept waiting on something going wrong. It didn't seem real. It seemed that all I knew was prison and it now felt strange to be leaving it all behind. My mind raced back to the time I was in Shotts and I was told about an old guy who had completed a 23 year sentence. He told the staff he didn't want to leave prison. He wanted to stay inside. Most of his time had been spent in the segregation unit. As he didn't like mixing with other prisoners, he was anxious and paranoid; he was let out for a week and killed himself. He couldn't cope. So 'what have I got to moan about' I asked myself; then I realised that it doesn't matter how long you have been inside, it affects everyone in different ways.

In my final week I arranged a visit for my family and I wanted to see my daughter before I went back to England. I wanted to give her a painting I had made for her. I had finished paintings for all my family although one I had completed for my little brother had gone missing from the art room. I had intended to give it to him at that visit. It was a good visit. I held back my emotions and tried to keep the visit light-hearted but everyone was feeling it. I said my goodbyes. It was like we would never see each other again. I knew inside this wasn't the case, but the unsaid things between us were as deep as deepest trench in the Atlantic Ocean. Finally after over two and a half years of solitude, pain, suffering, with the occasional light hearted interlude, my day came to leave prison. I didn't sleep all night and was shattered in the morning. I had two sports bags and one bin bag and a guitar, these were my worldly possessions. I had given everything else that I couldn't carry away, even my DVD player to other prisoners. On my way to the reception I kept thinking I wouldn't be let out, that the parole would be revoked. I stood outside the supervisor's office waiting on the paperwork to be sorted. I scared. I remember that at the same time, I had been waiting for my friend to turn up; I asked another prisoner where he was as I hadn't seen him for a few days. As this was during the week, he was supposed to have returned the previous weekend from his home leave. I was told that he had been asked to smuggle drugs into the prison. This was quite common and almost everyone was asked to do it. If you refused they tried to intimidate you or members of your family to force you to do it. As my family were not in the same social circle as these people and I had no history in housing estates in Scotland, I was not a target for this. However it was very common and even prisoner officers were not immune to this. My friend had used some of the drugs apparently, and had been tracked down and had his face cut open with an open razor, and had been too scared even to return to prison. When he was eventually caught, he received six months in a maximum security prison. I knew he had brought this on himself, and had been stupid, but this was yet another reason I had to get out. I needed to get away from these crazy bastards for my own sanity. At the supervisor's office, I signed the forms and had to wait another agonising hour for the driver to arrive. I was eventually, with little fanfare, and no welcome committee let out; I didn't relax until I had my feet on the train and it was moving away from the station. As I boarded the train and looked for an empty seat I finally gave out a sigh of relief. I was free.

Chapter 21

LIFE ON THE OUTSIDE, PAROLE.

I arrived in my girlfriend's home town and called her to arrange a meeting to sort out our differences. She was busy, too busy to see me. This was a blow, and just another disappointment I had to face. I thought she would be there waiting for me. After months of asking her to be truthful with me, she admitted she had been having a relationship with someone else. I knew myself I couldn't wait as long as that without at least a hug from another person. I tried to put the disappointment behind me and move on but it was difficult. Eventually we had a long discussion and it turned out that I had pushed her away by not writing to her; or when I did, I usually told her not to wait for me, and this had been too much for her. She assumed I had moved on, and wanted to move on too. It had been as much my fault as hers, and we realised this and tried again to make it work, and thankfully it did.

On my release, I tried frantically to find a job, even cleaning, but my time in prison was a barrier to employment. I was banging my head against a brick wall. The Rehabilitation of Offenders Act that the prison staff talked about didn't work on the outside. When the background checks were returned from a potential employer, it always said the same – no thanks. I felt discriminated against despite qualifications, ability, training and competence. I had no chance of getting a job from the people that were ignorant and unaware that ex-prisoners aren't animals nor are we all dangerous. More employers should receive appropriate guidance and training in legislation relating to the employment of ex- offenders and their rehabilitation but it's easier to ignore than address this. All my dreams, my thoughts and hopes were slowly turning to anger at the world around me. I did come out with a built-up frustration. I wasn't properly prepared for this. I desperately wanted out but there was a fear of living out here.

In prison, the pettiness of the rules breaks you down, but you have no need to think for yourself, everything is decided for you. While at first this is a punishment, eventually you depend on it for a sense of identity, purpose and safety. You learn to live with rules and regulations and forget what it's like to live life normally. I tried to get some voluntary work. So I filled in the necessary paper work however, because of my time in prison, I was turned down. One job I was trying to get involved working with young offenders. I was told I would be perfect for this but it would be up to the managing director who was an ex police commissioner. I didn't get it and the explanation was that they needed to protect young people. I was a very angry person and didn't know how to channel this anger and make it positive. I had thought my punishment was over, I was wrong.

On one occasion my girlfriend and I were having an argument at her flat and one of the male housemates came out and was trying to calm me down. I told him to go away, that I would destroy him. At that time I was so angry I would have taken anyone on. I was getting angry at everyone. Usually I would take offence from a small thing like a comment that others thought was funny. I wasn't drinking, doing drugs so what was wrong with me? My doctor put me on anti-depressants. I took them for three days and felt like a zombie and as if I had a hangover. Every day it took me till late afternoon before I would do anything. The migraines returned. I was frustrated and didn't know what to do. After around 14 months, I was offered a small comfortable flat. My neighbours were mostly retired, so it was quiet. I wanted a quiet life. I moved into the flat right away with only a bed and one two-seater couch. The lodge I had stayed in while homeless provided a fridge and a cooker and I received the rest of what I needed after a little time. I loved the freedom of this.

Although I was out of prison I was still experiencing stress because I had to make decisions for myself. That's the hardest to deal with when you are released, even though it was painful and humiliating to be at the mercy of sadistic guards, and even more sadistic prisoners, it had become safe. On the outside, having to think, act and decide things for myself was very difficult and very scary. I truly think this is one reason why rates of reconviction are so high among newly released prisoners, although there are other reasons, like lack of a job, stigma of having been inside making finding a job very difficult. Prison really does make it clear that society is very unfair, very divisive, and very hierarchical. The confinement where every action and thought is controlled becomes 'safe' and when people are scared they tend to do what's routine.

As a condition of my parole, I had to attend a probation officer's appointments on a weekly basis and tell them everything I was doing in the week before each visit. During these meetings they would ask me what I had been doing to pass the time, what I was doing for work and if I had any paper work to prove this. They were interested in minor things like what my hobbies had been, and perhaps more importantly, who I was associating with and I believed that they mixed in the wrong circles, did these associates drink or use drugs. They were interested in whether I used drugs and asked if I had been in trouble since we last met. They asked very personal questions about my love life and whether it affected me and my emotional state. They would enquire about my family, ask about my accommodation, and ask if I was in my opinion eating healthily. They wanted to know if I had been feeling anxious and paranoid, and did I think I had to talk to someone about this. I had of course felt anxious, but this was not the time to share this, I thought, shit if I say anything a Psychiatric Nurse would be force feeding me powerful anti psychotic drugs. I had no desire to look or sound mentally ill by taking powerful medication, or to become double incontinent and sit dribbling while looking blankly into space, a thing that happened with alarming regularity to ex prisoners in my experience.

It was not all bad though and I could see within this interview that there was care within this control. They asked if I had prepared a speech for job interviews and asked how I would handle the question about prison and how it affected me. They were also interested in my opinions of the week-long training outdoor exercise I had been on prior to my release. The governor I later heard had written to my family and had asked them if they thought that this week long excursion had helped me.

I started to furnish my new flat just the way I wanted, and I was finding out that life on the outside was not all I had imagined and dreamt of while I was in my cell. And to be honest I had become a pain in the arse as I had to have everything just so, for example my clothes had to be in a certain order. Inside, in my own cell, everything had a place and I could tell if anything had been moved. I could tell immediately if someone was in my cell, and if anything had been moved or taken. Prison does make you hyper vigilant, and this constant state of watching, looking out for constant threat of violence, or having something stolen, or having someone challenge you to a fight, is stressful, and the jail head skills required to survive inside are totally useless on the outside, and just made me feel even more alienated, more detached, and more like a prisoner, even now I was free! I didn't have many people in to visit. It was to be a while before it felt like anything other than a prison cell and it was to be a while before that would change.

I still found it difficult to cope with being around too many people so I didn't stay long when I went out. When I did go out it was usually to the beach or park on my own. I still did not trust people, and looking back I was pretty much acting like a wounded animal, I would bite when anyone came near me, but all I really wanted, what I truly needed was care, compassion and understanding. But I was not able to think rationally when I was first out. I still had my 'jail head' on. Taking this off, losing this set of attitudes and behaviours that had become essential to survival inside were causing me to be a prisoner on the outside.

Having paid my debt to society, finding a job, earning my own money, and becoming a proper citizen was difficult. I found that having to declare my time in prison made the possibility of an interview impossible, and when I was interviewed I was still not able to feel that I was anything other than 'guilty' of something. It's like Kafka's book 'The Trial'; in this book the accused was put on trial, but he was never told what he was guilty of; he was guilty of being accused, and this nightmare world expressed so beautifully how I was feeling. I was guilty of having been a prisoner. No one was caring what I had done time for; all they cared about was that I was 'dirty', and tainted; they were worried that I was potentially contagious, that I would corrupt the 'innocent' just by being in their presence.

How convicts are written about and described in newspapers, and popular films and TV dramas is really how most people learn about prison, and it scares them, and rightly so. However they have no idea that underneath the stigma prisoners are people with feelings. Becoming 'normal' and productive was difficult as the game was rigged, the rules only applied to 'clean' uncontaminated non prisoners. I would always be an ex offender, and ex con, someone who had done time. I would be seen like that, and people would feel certain things about me. I had no control over that. But the attitude society has about crime, punishment and rehabilitation, where all lines are blurred, and the fact that we cannot as a society decide whether we want to punish or rehabilitate people who are found guilty of crimes, means that we are neglecting to include citizens who could make a difference, who can contribute positively, and who are still, when all's said and done, people, just like you.

I felt guilty and expected to be judged, and often did not even get an interview for jobs that I would have been offered easily before my sentence. I couldn't get them to see the real me, the hard working man, willing to work. Before prison I was confident; I had everything I needed to be a normal productive citizen. I could get a job anywhere; I could do anything I chose to do within reason. However ordinary people don't like ex offenders, they are frightened. I still can't find a job, I don't go out as I have no money, I don't mix with people as I trust no one. My life really has been turned upside down. I have received so many rejection letters from prospective employers, written and posted countless CV's, all to no avail. I've been put down, and let down so many times that I feel beaten, but I still get up every morning and say it's a new day. I feel confident that things must change no matter what, despite my moans, despite me writing all of this down, I have my freedom. Despite all the knocks to my confidence, all of the changes that happened to me, I'm out of prison; I decide what happens to me.

Being inside prison is a brutal life changing environment. Before I entered prison, I was a person with a first and last name who was to become just another number on a prison wing. I was at first frightened by the whole prison system as I was weak in body and mind and in this state I was eventually battered and beaten into submission. I was lost in this new environment and I was abused, frightened, and preyed on by those who had become used to the brutality, and had lost all ability to connect and feel empathy for another human being. After settling in, and becoming used to the madness and the routine brutality that I witnessed daily, I had no choice but to fight back, and not try to be seen as a good person.

Being nice and polite are normal characteristics that go a long way on the outside but have no currency on the inside. I had to become just like other prisoners. I needed to be part of the way it was and always will be in prison, harsh with its own rules, which to an outsider unused to it, as a 'topsy turvey' world, with everything almost reversed. Politeness and civility, and speaking without swearing were seen as major weaknesses. I took me a long time to learn how to hide emotion. To show weakness was to invite trouble. In a situation where it was me against another, even if I felt sorry for the person, I would strike the first blow to settle the issue, and to send a powerful signal that I was just like they were, brutal, strong, and able to fight for my place in the hierarchy. I knew that at times others were stronger than me so I trained myself to be strong to hit hard and this led me to become what I hated them for when I first came into prison. This made me angry, resentful, fearful, and was exhausting. This anger, this 'jail head', this 'mask' eventually became permanent and I carried it to the outside not knowing how to take it off. Just after my release I found myself in a fight with a guy who had made some comment when I was engaged in an argument with my girlfriend. Without even stopping to think about the consequences, I picked him up off the ground and whispered in his ear that I would find out where he lived and kill him in his sleep. He was so scared I put him down, and in looking at his fear, I recognised what he was feeling and remembered that I was out now. I didn't need to be like this anymore. I had become a bully, this was what being inside had done to me, and I needed to lose this identity which had served me well on the inside, or I would be returning to prison. Everything I had learned inside, I had to unlearn now and start all over again. I had to get the true me back and I didn't know how to start undoing what they had done to me. I had left prison still a prisoner. How I had become like this was not just down to how I was treated by the other prisoners, but the prison officers as well. They say time heals all, and in many respects this is of course a truism. I have changed although I think I'm still alert and I'm still conscious of my surroundings but I have calmed down now and love peace and quiet. I finally lost the 'jail head', but the fear that it might still lurk deep within my psyche scares me. I have returned to more peaceful and life affirming pursuits, I now love to paint using oils and watercolours, I enjoy playing my guitar and I sit at times and remember how lucky I am. I survived the horror of times past and often find time to stop to think of just how lucky I am to have my family and, ah yes, my freedom.

It is commonly said that time heals everything. Maybe it just dulls the pain of past events, of the bad or good things we have lived through. It is a tough world and people can be cruel without meaning to be inside prison, and outside prison. I regret parts of my life, and there are things I really wish I had never done. We all have these things we regret, things that keep us awake at night unable to sleep, unable to forgive ourselves, and worried about how we are perceived by others. I know life inside would have be unbearable if I had not been able to rely on the help and support of my family. Nothing I could write here could demonstrate what a difference they made to my life, just to have that contact and support. So to them I dedicate this book.

About the Author

Wallace was an ordinary guy in his mid thirties working as a full time carer, and a part time nighclub doorman when a car accident changed his life forever. Convicted of dangerous driving which resulted in a death, he was sentenced to five years in prison. His book documents his experiences as he gained the skillls necessary to surive in prison. His unique insight as a non criminal locked up with lifers, rapists, and drug dealers, and easy writing style highlights his desire to lose the skills he needed to surivive inside and his struggle to stay out of prison on his release.

www.ingramcontent.com/pod-product-compliance
Lightning Source LLC
Chambersburg PA
CBHW051426280526
45785CB00003B/1182